Lakeland's Pioneer Rock-Climbers

Based on the Visitors' Books of the
Tysons of Wasdale Head, 1876-86.

D1407499

by
Herbert & Mary Jackson

Dalesman Books
1980

The Dalesman Publishing Company Ltd.,
Clapham (via Lancaster), North Yorkshire

First published 1980

ISBN: 0 85206 601 5

Printed by Galava Printing Company Limited, Nelson, Lancashire.

Contents

Cover painting by Tim Cowdell.

Photographs in the text on pages 49-56 and 105-112.

Introduction

Some years ago Mrs Hannah Briggs, nee Williamson, of Maryport, gave to us visitors' books relating to the years 1876-86, at one time the property of Mr and Mrs Thomas Tyson, Row Farm, Wasdale Head. The Williamsons and the Tysons were both old Maryport families and related by marriage. After a careful examination we were thrilled to discover that, not only did the books contain the names and addresses of those who stayed with the Tysons as paying guests, but also written in the books were detailed descriptions of rock climbs in the Wasdale area. These are in the handwriting of Walter Parry Haskett-Smith, known as the 'Father of English Climbers', and of many other eminent pioneers of rock climbing in the English Lake District.

The information, we believe, will add greatly to the history of rock climbing and tourism in the Lake District. Almost every page contains written comments from national figures in many fields. The visitors' books for the period 1876-86, reproduced here, contain descriptions of climbs and walks in Cumbria, poems, pen and ink sketches, and interesting comments.

The latter years of the 19th century have been referred to as the 'golden age of climbing' in the Lake District, with the main centre being the Wasdale Head area. Much has been written of this period and of the influence of that great Cumbrian character, Will Ritson, mine host of the Huntsman Inn at Wasdale, and of the rock climbing fraternity who stayed there. These hitherto unpublished visitors' books of the Tysons show clearly that during this part of the 19th century the Row Farm guest house was the major centre for climbers, fell walkers and travellers.

This was a time when the Lake District was becoming a popular resort. The greatest attraction for tourists was the unspoiled quality of the countryside. Even in those far-off days, hotels, guest houses and farm houses were busy in summer and during the Christmas, Easter and Whitsuntide holidays. The coming of the railways in the mid part of the 19th century greatly added to the number of visitors. Railway companies from the 1860s onwards ran weekend excursions from the industrial towns of the north to the Lake District. The railways, by bringing holiday-makers in ever increasing numbers, caused large hotels to be built, the 'Windermere', 'Grange' and 'Keswick' hotels to name but a few. This was followed by the building of smaller hotels and the conversion of private houses into guest houses, together with the use of farm houses for providing facilities for the traveller and tourist. By 1877 Grasmere had 18 places offering accommodation.

Such firms as Riggs of Windermere provided, as part of their hotel services, their own coaches and coach services. They also maintained fleets of carriages for hire. A single horse conveyance cost £1 for a day's hire, with a further 2½p per hour or 25p per day for the driver. In one year 21,480 carriages passed and re-passed by Troutbeck Bridge on the Windermere-Ambleside road and over 15,000 paid toll on the road section nearer Grasmere and Keswick. Horse drawn coaches ran daily services from Windermere railway station to Keswick, Cockermouth and Hawkshead.

In the last century fell walking was a serious matter. Even à simple valley walk needed thought and preparation. A holiday in the Lake District in the 1870s meant a stay in an hotel, inn or farmhouse for some weeks. In a guide book published at this time, the following advice is given regarding dress and baggage: 'What is needed for a lady and gentleman is a fair sized portmanteau, a rail or coach, and the bag can easily be carried on a horse or in a mountain cart. Thick boots are essential and plenty of wraps and waterproofs. The walker is warm in the daytime, but near the lakes, quite cool in the evening, so a light shawl should be carried on afternoon excursions......'

What today we term as fells were then called mountains, and ponies could be hired for mountain excursions at 37½p per day. For the ascent of Coniston Old Man the charge for a pony and guide was 55p, for Scafell from Dungeon Ghyll 90p, and from Wasdale Head 50p. Fell walking rapidly became popular; often parties of students from the two senior universities stayed at hotels and farm houses, combining rock climbing in the daytime with intellectual discussions in the evenings.

Wasdale Head, to become the climbing centre of Lakeland, was in the latter part of the 19th century a small hamlet situated at the head of Wastwater. It lies 12 miles north-east of Ravenglass and 16 miles east-by-south of Egremont, which is the nearest town. There was a woollen manufactory, a corn-mill and a bobbin manufactory. The proximity of Scafell, the Napes Ridges on Great Gable and Pillar Rock made Wasdale a natural climbing centre. For the fell walkers, as opposed to the climbers, there were the Scafells, Great Gable, Kirkfell and the round of Pillar, Red Pike and Yewbarrow. In addition there were good walks by the side of Wastwater, the deepest of the lakes. Unfortunately, during this golden age of climbing, the rock climbers did not often commit their experiences to paper, making the Tysons' visitors' books all the more interesting. Of course, a visit to Wasdale Head meant a long walk or carriage ride from the nearest railway station. Not until 1875 was the narrow gauge railway line extended to Boot.

To Wasdale Head and the Tysons' tee-total farmhouse came parties of visitors from London, Manchester, Liverpool, Leeds, Bradford and the North-East as well as from the universities. The pioneer climbers were principally gentlemen of the upper and middle classes who were endowed with a spirit of adventure. The dangers of the new sport of rock climbing provided fulfillment, enjoyment and satisfaction. Many led busy family and professional lives far away from Wasdale. Usually climbing was limited to the holiday periods. The early rock climbers learned their skills on Pillar Rock, Scafell Crag and the Napes face of Great Gable.

The Tysons themselves were a family of great antiquity, with a special affinity for the Lake District. The name is of Norwegian derivation and was spelled Tyssen, meaning Son of Ty or Tyr, the Sword God. In 1066 a Gilbert Tyson fell at King Harold's side at the Battle of Hastings. Another member of the family, Adam Tyson, appears as one of the taxers for Braithwaite in 1332. It is known that Tysons were well established at Irton, Birker, Egremont and in Eskdale by the reign of Elizabeth I. In 1578 a John Tyson was one of the tenants at Wasdale Head, and in the 17th century the family became more strongly represented there and in Nether Wasdale. By the early 18th century their farmsteads in Nether Wasdale were Greendale, Strand and Buckbarrow; there was a Henry Tyson at Greendale in 1728. In Eskdale, Tysons were at Row Head, Hollins and Christ Cliff for long periods. Later they became established in West Cumberland, the Langdales and southward to Whicham and Millom, to Ulpha and Broughton, to Kirkby, Dalton, Colton and Ulverston. The family have been domiciled in the Furness area for centuries. Such families have been the backbone of this county right up to the present day.

Under the guidance of Tom and Annie Tyson, the house at Row Farm became a guest house. The bedrooms were comfortable; there was good home cooking. Whatever hour of the day or night that visitors arrived, they were assured of a warm welcome from Mrs Tyson and her husband. Visitors to Row Farm could be divided into the following categories—the rock climbing fraternity, the fell walkers and family parties, all of whom spent holidays ranging from a few days to several weeks. During the ten years which concern us the Tysons received into their home, as paying guests, people from all over the British Isles and from almost a score of foreign countries. This was a fantastic achievement in the 19th century, for travel was slow, difficult and expensive.

The final category of regular visitors to Row Farm, particularly on Sundays, were local people living within a radius of thirty miles, who arrived either on foot or by horse and trap to enjoy one of Annie Tyson's almost legendary farmhouse teas. She was famous for ham and eggs and gooseberry pie. In the summer months Annie Tyson and her daughters found it difficult to cope with the ever increasing demand for the good food they provided at reasonable prices.

Throughout the Visitors' Books tributes to the Tysons' hospitality appear and we think are best summarised by the following entries. Firstly, an entry in September 1876:-

'Try not Ritson's, an old man said,
You'll get hard fare and harder bed,
So move a little higher,
Only at Tyson's will you meet,
No food or bed that is not sweet,
So sit beside his fire.'

Secondly, on June 3rd, 1879:-

'O, Traveller, rest at Mrs Tyson's,
Her ham is good, the eggs are nice uns,
When I was here, our numbers plenty,
Came to exactly two and twenty,
The old hens laid till sore distressed,
Our hostess kind, we found and able,
As she should be, who owns Great Gable.'

Let us look into the backgrounds of Thomas and Mary Ann (Annie) Tyson. Husband Thomas was born in King Street, Maryport, Cumberland, in 1833. The census returns of 1841 show that his father, William, was then aged 40 years and a plumber by trade. His mother, Ann, was 35 years old. Thomas is shown as the eldest child of the family, aged eight years. His brother, John, was two, and sister Sarah, then the youngest member of the family, was just one year old.

Maryport, where Thomas Tyson was born, had been created in 1749 by Humphrey Senhouse, Lord of the Manor of Netherhall, and so named in honour of his wife, Mary. The new town was expanding rapidly and in the 1830s had a population of almost 4,000. Its wealth lay in the coal, mined in the surrounding countryside, most of which was exported to Ireland. Thomas' home in King Street was only a few yards away from the busy harbours and shipbuilding yards. It was near to his home in 1837 that the first broadside launch in Maryport was made — the ship was the 'Airey', built by John Peat.

The roads in and out of the town were little better than rough country lanes. The traditional method of road repair was to tumble a cartload of stones into the biggest holes and wait for the traffic to flatten them down. In spite of this, the 'Royal Sailor' stage coach ran daily from Carlisle, via Wigton and Allonby to Maryport, entering Maryport at the northern end of King Street. The journey from Carlisle to Maryport took four to five hours, while the return journey took six hours. A carrier service to Whitehaven was provided by John Clark; this ran on Mondays, Thursdays and Saturdays, leaving Maryport at 1 p.m. and returning the same day. George Stephenson, the railway pioneer, visited Maryport in 1836 and stayed at the Golden Lion Hotel. The outcome of this visit was the opening of the first section of the Maryport and Carlisle Railway, from Maryport to Arkleby in 1840. The line from Maryport to Carlisle was opened for traffic in 1845, when Thomas was 12 years old. The express train completed the journey in 70 minutes.

William and Ann Tyson must have been fairly prosperous, for King Street, as well as being the busy main road to Allonby and Carlisle, was one of the better residential districts of the town. During Thomas' boyhood the streets were lit by gas and he grew up near the bustle of the harbour, with its foreign boats and their crews. At the northern end of the town, past the gas works, there lay the Sea Brows, with fields above and below, providing a natural playground for the local boys and girls. It was this environment which attracted Thomas to the open air life he was to enjoy in Wasdale in his later years.

Thomas is mentioned in an amusing story written by Walter Parry Haskett-Smith, who relates that a well-known character at Wasdale Head was a certain Tommy Tompson. One day, Haskett-Smith and John Robinson of Lorton met Tompson when they were out walking. While the three were talking, Tom Tyson passed in the distance and they spoke of his crumpled ear. Tyson's account of it was that, years before, he had been on Gable Screes one winter's day, had lost his footing and slid a great distance down the steep, hard snowslope, grinding off most of his ear in the process. On Robinson referring to this, Tommy Tompson was very interested and said, with great simplicity, 'Was that the way of it! Wal! Wal! An' us ollas tho-at that ear was takken off by a cartwheel, when Tom was liggam drunk i' t' road'.

Mary Ann Tyson, during her busy years at Row Farm, became as noted earlier a legend in her lifetime for the hospitality she dispensed to visitors. She was the daughter of John and Isabella Williamson of Hudscales. Born in December 1828, Mary Ann Williamson was baptised in St Kentigern's Church, Caldbeck, by the curate, Rev. W. Pattinson, on January 4th, 1829. Her father, John, is described in the baptismal register as a farmer. Caldbeck is eight miles south-east of Wigton and less than two miles from Hudscales, where John Williamson was a substantial farmer. The nearest township to the Williamson farm was Hesket Newmarket, half a mile distant. The only place of worship in this small market centre in the early 19th century was the Quaker chapel, which was the reason that Mary Ann's baptism took place at Caldbeck church.

Hesket Newmarket, with the river Calder flowing close by, was a busy and prosperous place during Mary Ann's childhood. In addition to regular cattle and sheep sales, it had a weekly Friday market. The

9

local carrier Anthony Bowman was the principal link with the larger centres of population and journeyed each week to Wigton on Monday, Penrith on Tuesday and Carlisle on Saturday. Historically, Hesket Newmarket was of great interest. Pre-Roman remains had been found at Gillfoot and the main road through the town had been built by the Romans.

Brought up on her parents' farm on the Caldbeck fells, Mary Ann enjoyed a happy childhood. She attended the local school. Farm life agreed with her, so much so that on her marriage to Thomas she readily took up residence at Row Farm. In her days at Hudscales, Mary Ann would often see John Peel (1777-1854), the famous fox-hunter who lived at nearby Caldbeck. His name was perpetuated by Woodcock Graves in the best known of all hunting songs. Life at Hudscales was satisfying and proved an excellent training ground for her later years in South Cumberland.

1876

The initial entry in the visitors' books is dated September 1st, 1876 and reads as follows:

Carpenter.
Child.
T.P. Mulcaster.
W.V. Mulcaster.
B.F.F. Mulcaster, Benwell Park, Newcastle upon Tyne.
followed by

September 2..
Mr and Mrs E.K. Haywood, Great Crosby, Liverpool in company with the five preceding gentlemen, under the kind guidance and assistance of Mr R. Pendlebury, Broad Green, Liverpool, ascended the Pillar Rock. Enjoyed the five days here very much and have great pleasure in adding their testimony to the kindness and hospitality of the host and hostess, Mr and Mrs Tyson.

The concluding remarks in the introduction about the hospitality of the Tysons are reiterated innumerable times throughout the visitors' books. The news of good food and comfortable beds at Row Farm soon spread and brought about a constant influx of visitors.

August 28-September 6.
Maria Clutton, Wickham, Bishop's Rectory.
Lucy Collin and Ernest Collin, Saffron Walden, having been made most comfortable by Mr and Mrs Tyson, whether wet or dry have thoroughly enjoyed their ten days visit.

September 6.
W.I. Toye, Wellington College.
E.A.A. Spencer, Wellington College.

September 8.
Jas Thornton, Plymouth.
George Foster, Farnworth.
Samuel Rogers Farnworth.

Providence was kind to A. Holborn, Huyton and J.H. Spalding, Bromley in sending two gentlemen to the top of Scafell Pike to tell them of this most comfortable house.

T.J. Rone, A. Armitage, two Nottingham lambs, decidedly sheep-headed. N.B. Can confidently recommend the plum jam. After spending two days here we cannot speak too highly of Dame Tyson's kindness.

Mrs Briggs, Hensingham.
Mrs Dawson, Gosforth.
John Briggs, Hensingham.
Tom Tyson.
D.C. Embleton, Newcastle.
Charles Edward Beebor, London, experienced the kindest reception they have had in any part of the Lake District; they have to thank Mr and Mrs Tyson for their great attention to their comfort and hope to come again.
September 11.
Edward Stevens, London.
John Nelson, Whitehaven.
Joseph Gouldie, Leeds.
Thomas Watson, Wath Brow.
John Watson, Connaught.
John Varty, Newcastle.
This company arrived at Wasdale at William Ritson's and were served with drinks, but with all their entreaties could not get anything to eat, till they reached Dame Tyson's, where they were treated with every civility and a good dinner was found them.

Will Ritson was a colourful Lake District character. He was born in 1808 at Row Foot, Wasdale Head, which is the site of the present Wastwater Hotel but then was a small farmstead. At an early age he became huntsman to Mr Rawson of Wasdale Hall, then to Mr Huddleston of Gosforth. Later he formed and maintained a pack of his own.

Dinah, his wife, was a member of an ancient local family, the Fletchers of Nether Wasdale. In the middle of the last century Will Ritson, who lived with Dinah, his son and two servants at the farm, realised that some people derived enjoyment from walking up mountains. Thereupon he built a small wing on to his farmhouse, secured a drinking licence in 1856, called it the Huntsman Inn and fed his visitors with the traditional meal of Cumberland ham and eggs. The Huntsman Inn is now the annexe of the Wastwater Hotel and for well over a hundred years has been used by thousands of walkers and climbers.

Will, wrestler, huntsman, mountain guide and landlord, became widely known as a story-teller and wit. It was he who made the now legendary description of the Wasdale area as containing 'the highest mountain, the deepest lake, the smallest church and the biggest liar' in England.

Many distinguished people visited the Huntsman Inn at Wasdale Head to see this remarkable dalesman, of whom they had heard so much, and listened to his stories, as well as climbing the mountains not only for the exercise but for the breathtaking views from the summits. In the Huntsman's small kitchen, with its flagged floor and rough wooden benches, Ritson acted as landlord, waiter and customer. He held court with farmers, shepherds and visitors and was friendly with the famous, including Wordsworth and De Quincey. Invariably Ritson spoke in the broadest Cumbrian dialect. Will and Dinah retired from the Huntsman in 1879 and lived at Nicol Ground, Nether Wasdale, which is seven miles from Seascale. He died in 1890, aged 83, and is buried in the Nether Wasdale churchyard.

September 11.
After looking in vain for some time in Seascale ..... of anything comfortable in the way of lodgings. Then at Wasdale, we were delighted to find this 'haven of REST', where we experienced every kindness and attention from Dame Tyson. We depart in the hope of re-newing our acquaintance with her at some future time.
Robert Crotty, Dublin.
S. A. Crotty, Dublin.
Seascale was in the 19th century, as it is today, a popular sun bathing place, and until 1901 a township in the parish of Gosforth. The church of St Cuthbert was not built until 1890, and is of local red sandstone. It was formerly a chapel of ease to Gosforth.

Mr. C. R. Bree, M.D., of Colchester wrote an article entitled, 'The Natural History of Wastdale', a cutting of which following publication was inserted in the visitor's book of Dame Tyson. It is reproduced in full:-
Sterne tells us, in his 'Sentimental Journay', that he pities the man who can travel from Dan to Beersheba and say 'tis barren', and he continues; 'And so it is, and so is all the world, to him who will not cultivate the fruits it offers.'
Nothing can apparently be more barren as to animal life than your first impression of WASTDALE, and yet its fauna are well worth a line or two. I will preface what I have to say by a short description of the place.
Travellers to the Lakes are well acquainted with the locality, for most of them pay it a visit and pass through by Black Sail to Buttermere; but it is not generally known what a charming spot it is. Horses and walking are the only means of reaching WASTDALE on two sides, while the third way runs down to Drigg on the Furness Railway, thirteen miles. Coming from this latter place you pass the residence of Mr Musgrave deep down by the lake-side, near its lower end. You then come upon the lake-side, and run along a hilly road for three miles and a half, along the shores of WASTWATER. On the opposite side is the mountain called The Screes, which shows three or four rather wide patches of loose stones from the top to the bottom

13

of the mountain, and going straight into the lake at the bottom, where it is said to be two hundred and seventy fathoms deep, and is never frozen over in the sharpest weather. You pass on a mile above the bend of the lake, when you arrive at the inn of Mr Ritson and the COMFORTABLE LODGINGS OF MRS TYSON. While the latter lady is preparing dinner, just take a short climb to a rock she will point out for you on Kirk Fell, and there you will have a magnificent view. Straight before you there are about fifty cultivated fields, looking very green, and surrounded in the quaintest way by stone walls, with a crop of oats here and there, and at the bottom the head of WASTWATER, with The Screes beyond. To the left you catch a glimpse of the top of Scawfell Pikes, the highest point in England, but the principal part is hid by Lingmell. Further to the left you see the Great End, separating Scawfell from the well-known pass of Stye-Head; then, coming down towards you, is the fourth highest mountain in England, Gable-End, which, with Kirk Fell, upon which you are sitting, have been in the possession of our landlord's family for seven hundred years. To the right you see the commencement of the valley, which leads you through Black Sail to Borrowdale and Ennerdale. Further on is the Pillar Mountain, separated from Eagle's Cragg by Windy Gap; and the amphitheatre on the right is closed in by Red Cragg and Yewbarrow Mountains. From these hills two streams run down to the lake, of which more anon.

Such is WASTDALE, which belongs to the parish of St Bees, has thirty-four inhabitants, one of the smallest churches in England — with only eight pews, is twelve miles from a doctor, ten from a butcher or policeman, and if your horse loses a shoe you cannot have it renewed under thirteen and a half miles.

All this looks very like Skye, or some other place in the Hebrides, and yet it is in reality only fourteen miles over Sty-Head from Keswick. The people are well to do dalesmen, who make a good thing out of the various travellers during the summer, although their charges are moderate.

Well, as to the fauna of such a place. Foxes are numerous if not kept down, which they now are by a subscription pack of hounds, the expenses of which are borne by the dalesmen, and whose object is entirely that of destruction.

Mr Ritson, the landlord of the only Inn in the dale, assured me that in one year fifty-two lambs and sheep had been worried, by the foxes. The hunting is done on foot chiefly, and long days and distances over the tops of mountains are the order of the day. Next to foxes the animal most persecuted is 'The Sweet Mart', which is the common Marten, and called 'Sweet' to distinguish it from the 'fou-mart', which is very offensive, as its name signifies. These martens are injurious, so the shepherds say, to young lambs. They live in holes among the rocks, high up among the mountains, where they have no doubt been located since their creation. They feed also upon the few hares and rabbits or rats and mice found in the

14

mountains. They are hunted with Scotch Terriers, which are taught to draw them like a badger. Hares and rabbits are not numerous, as they have many foes; but rats and mice occur in favourable localities.

The mountain sheep is well-known to be a distinct breed. Every mountain is stocked with the sheep it will carry, and is thus let to the tenant, who is bound to leave as many sheep on the mountain when he leaves it. Each sheep knows its own mountain well enough, though the rascals show their cleverness in jumping walls and straying away from home. Each sheep has its own resting place, to which it returns to sleep every night; and the best mutton comes from those sheep who live among the high mountain rocks, which, to a traveller's eye, are bare of food. It is very amusing to see the working of the Colley Dog; black and white seems to be that which obtains most. At a word or signal from its master it will go anywhere and do anything. They are, some of them, of very irritable temper, which renders it advisable to be on good terms with them. A few cattle and horses are kept in the dale, and there were a couple of black wise looking cats in the house in which we lodged.

With regard to birds I saw the dipper flitting along the stream of Red-beck, now and then alighting on a rock in the water, and saluting me with a series of good natured bobs. The wheatear and its young were also there, as was the everlasting pied-wagtail and a large pipit, which I did not make out. I also identified a grey flycatcher, blackbirds and thrushes, robin red-breast, chaffinches, swallows (House martins), but I could not see any house sparrows. Flying over the lake I saw some herring-gulls, and a pair of larger gulls with black wings and dark slate coloured plumage, which I thought might be our large skua (lestris catarrhactes). I saw one also in the valley. A gentleman named Grant told me he saw, what from his description, I assumed to be, the common buzzard and my landlord informed me that some owls had possession of the rocks on Lingmell a year or two ago.

The two rivers which drain the mountains above mentioned and run into WASTWATER are full of small trout and parr. During the only spate we had in the week, I caught a trout nearly three quarters of a pound with the worm. Is parr distinct from the samlet, and is the former, without doubt, the young of the salmon? When we were in WASTDALE, the end of August, these parr were from one inch to three inches long—a very small fish at that time of year. That salmon come up to the waterfall near our lodgings, about a mile from the lake, there is no doubt. In great floods they are often washed into the meadows, on to banks of the rivers, and being out of season they are boiled up for pigs. In the Irt, which takes away the water of WASTWATER to the sea, I saw a salmon rise of about six or seven pounds, as we passed along the road, about half way between Drigg and WASTDALE. I saw nothing like the pink form of young salmon; and I can hardly imagine that salmon spawn emitted in November, or at the latest March, should not produce fish which would be larger

15

than any I saw in August. You are aware that Couch writes of the parr as a distinct fish on its own account, having occurred in rivers where no salmon are ever seen. At all events, the magistrates who act for WASTWATER will fine anyone £10 who is known to have a parr or a branlin as the natives call them, in his possession. A Mr Parnaby, who has established a large aquarium in Borrowdale, and who hires the fishing in WASTWATER, must be able to answer this question. There is nothing in WASTWATER but charr, salmon, trout, and eels, the absence of pike and perch being singular.

I cannot conclude this short notice without a word about poor Mr Barnard, who was lost in the mountain, and whose remains, I see by today's Times (September 11th) have been found near Pillar Rock within two miles from WASTWATER. Mr Pendlebury, Senior Wrangler and Mathematical Lecturer at St John's, Cambridge, who is a capital mountaineer, was in the same house with us. I saw him the evening he arrived, and he told me his firm conviction was that the lost man was under Pillar Rock. He went with a party next morning, but came back without success. The place has been examined to my certain knowledge four or five times, and yet near there he was concealed, as the papers will doubtless tell us.

P.S. I have just seen a fine Manx Shearwater killed on the telegraph wires near here.

September 13.
Frederick Robinson, London.
Everything very clean and attention good.

September 14.
C. R. Barker, Leamington College.
Received the greatest kindness and hospitality at Dame Tysons.

C. A. Parker. MB.
Mrs Parker.
Mr Reynolds, Knaresborough, Yorkshire.
S. Omerod, South Australia.
G. I. Booth, Rochdale.

September 15.
John Green, H.P.C., Manchester.
Gordon Smith, Sidney Sussex College, Cambridge.
James Cutter, Leeds.

September 18.
Mr and Mrs T. Knowles, Eccles.

Charles Sanger, Westcott.
E.P. Sanger, London.
This latter gentleman is young and has carved his name on a piece of slate to leave on the top of the Pillar Rock.

Pillar is mentioned in Hutchinson's 'History of Cumberland', published in 1794. Wordsworth's poem, 'The Brothers', published in 1820, gained some notoriety for Pillar, as it tells the story of a

*shepherd who was killed in a fall from the crag. The first authentic
account of a Lake District rock climbing ascent was in fact that of
Pillar by John Atkinson in 1826. The feat received a good deal of
prominence in the local press.*

September 18.
Try not Ritsons an old man said,
You'll get hard fare and harder bed,
So move a little higher,
Only at Tyson's will you meet,
No food or bed that is not sweet,
So sit beside his fire.
H. Pears, Addlestone, Surrey.
*The atmosphere at Row Farm must have stimulated the poetic
impulse of many of the visitors. Throughout the entries there are
numerous instances.*

September 19.
H. Ley and wife, Sellack Vicarage, Ross, Herefordshire.
Spent four days here, very comfortably; sorry to go; hope to pay
another visit to our kind host and hostess.
September 20.
T.M. King, Windermere.
H.R. King, Windermere.
H.P. Mason, Kirkby Stephen.
Mary Mason.
September 21.
Arthur Jolly, London.
September 28.
The undersigned left Victoria Hotel, Buttermere, at 10 o'clock for
Scale Force, from there by Scarf Gap and Black Sail for Wasdale
Head where he arrived footsore and tired and was kindly treated by
Dame Tyson.
Signed. W. London.
*Buttermere, on the Sail Beck, between Crummock Water and the
lake of its own name, is nine miles from Keswick. The scenery is
magnificent, especially on the west side, where a long range of
mountain slopes rising to the lofty ridges of High Crag [2,443 ft] and
High Stile [2,643 ft] stretch from end to end of the lake. At the head
of Buttermere lie the high passes of Black Sail and Scarth Gap.*

September 29 to October 1.
E.R. and M. Wharton, Oxford.
October 3.
A.B. Dickson, Abbots Reading, Haverthwaite.
A.M. Gregson, Moorchurch, Kent Bank.

17

October 7.
J.W. Berry, Norton, Stockton on Tees.
October 25.
Mr and Mrs. Dixon, Fish Hotel, Buttermere.
Splendid weather.

The Fish Hotel is as popular today with visitors as it was then. A stream flows past the hotel, through the intervening meadows, connecting Buttermere Lake, which is about one and a half miles in length and nearly half a mile broad, with Crummock Water, which is much larger. The latter is about two and a half miles long and half a mile across; it receives the waters of Scale Force.

1877

March 30.
H.F. Blair, Manchester.
F. Hulton, Manchester.
F.W. Haywood, Manchester.
April 2.
C.H. Dibb, Bradford.
Alfred Crebbin, Bradford.
B. Entwistle.
J.S. Davy.
E.F. Ames.
T.E. Davy.
April 4.
W.H. Ferguson, Christ Church, Oxford.
March 24 to April 10.
John Mason, Pembroke College, Cambridge.
Arthur Stanley Butler, Exon College, Oxon.
Tunstall Smith, St Johns College, Cambridge.
Henry R. King, Exeter College, Oxford.
April 22.
John P. Hare, walked from Keswick via Sty Head Pass. Very comfortable bed, tea and breakfast.
Sty Head Pass, the route from Borrowdale to Wasdale Head, has been used by travellers from time immemorial. One notable resident of Keswick, the poet Coleridge, set out to climb Scafell in August 1802. Using a brush handle as an alpenstock and carrying on his back a bag containing food and writing material, he climbed via Sty Head Pass to the summit of Scafell, becoming the first of our national poets to achieve this feat.
April 25.
C.R. Barker, M.A., Leamington College.
Errol Smith, Edinburgh University.
Entertained by Dame Tyson with her usual kindness.
May 2.
Rev. H.S. Collinder.
Brathay on way to Ennerdale.
Brathay Hall, at the northern end of Windermere on the road from

Ambleside to Coniston, had a distinguished visitor in 1806. The painter, Constable spent two months as a guest of the Hardens at the hall, sketching. One of his sketches of Great Langdale included a non-existent lake at the foot of the Langdale Pikes.

May 7.
Mr and Mrs Norman Wrigley, Huddersfield.
Miss Wrigley.
Miss Barton.
K.W. Girdlestone.
S.A. Ponsonby.
C.G. Romaine.
H.L.S. MacDonald.
J.E.Judson.
William T. Cotterill, Sheffield.
May 10.
Charles H. Stacey, Rawmoor, Sheffield.
Arrived via Coniston.
Coniston Lake lies to the west of Windermere and parallel to it, but is much shorter and narrower, with its head in the mountains and its foot practically in lowland country. In 1871 John Ruskin, art critic, painter and social reformer, came to make his permanent home at Brantwood, which lies at the head of the lake facing Coniston Old Man.

May 16 to 17.
James R. Anderson, Alderley Edge, Manchester.
Jane L. Anderson, Maulesbank, Carnoustie, Dundee.
May 22.
John Turnbull, Leeds.
Parson Turnbull, Leeds.
John Robinson, Leeds.

I am gai, I am poete, I am well,
In Bradford, of Yorkshire, I dwell,
And I sing tra, la, la,
And I love my mama,
And ze English, I speak him quite well.
Signed, W.B.G.
May 24.
E. Hulton, Preston.
H.E.------, Bradford.
Francis. E. Wilson, Birkdale, Southport.
Mr. W. Binyon, Malvern.
M. Porter, Holmrook.
A.B. Ashburner, 35 Huskisson Street, Liverpool.
May 26.
David Smith, Manchester.
James Hoy.

William Henry Johnson.
John E. Rhodes.
John W. Roberts.
Herbert Harrison, Manchester.
June 20.
Mr and Mrs Utt---, Norwich.
Mr and Mrs -ippet, Liverpool.
Miss Hipkin, Norwich.
G.H. Hipkin, Honingham, Norwich.
June 21.
John Beavaid, Toxteth Park, Liverpool.
The comments are in shorthand, and translate as follows:
Left this hospitable cheer accompanied by William Alfred Todd.
-- of Scafell Pike in less than two and a half hours through the thick
mist and heavy rain; on reaching the summit they were however
gratified with a most extensive panoramic view of the surrounding
country. -- having been replaced by the sunshine after spending
about half an hour on the summit, we crossed sundry mountains to
Great Langdale where the writer parted with the company of ------
by Borrowdale and Sty Head Pass, having walked in descent of about
32 miles. --- and would also bear our testimony to the kind attention
and courtesy of Dame Tyson. W.A. Todd left on Monday the 25th.
(Some of the writing is too faded to translate).
June 28.
Mr and Mrs G.B. Livens, Newcastle upon Tyne, came over the top
of Kirk Fell from Ennerdale the previous day and can confidently
recommend this route to all lovers of loose stones and rocks big
and little. A strong pair of boots will be necessary to bring you
whole-foot to W. Tysons.
George Hornblower, Birkenhead.
There is a great similarity between the scenery surrounding Enner-
dale Lake and that of Wastwater. To reach Wastwater from
Ennerdale, the best route is from the upper part of the valley over
Black Sail Pass, beyond which rises Kirk Fell [2631 ft].

June 30.
Herbert Mansergh, Birkenhead.
Ascended the Pillar by Black Sail before breakfast. Down at
9.30 a.m.
Pillar Mountain [2927 ft], on the southern side of the Ennerdale
valley, incorporates the Pillar Rock, which was considered inaccess-
ible until it was first climbed in 1826.

July 1.
S.M. Gregson.
M.H. Gregson.
Hartley. P. Kayll, The Elms, Sunderland.
Andrew J. Kayll, Brasenose College, Oxford.
Alfred Edge Kayll, Park House, Sunderland.

Sten Schale, Engeneer, Stockholm, Sweden.
Rev. J. Midgley, Leeds.
Henry Kirk, Workington.
C.J. Valentine, Workington.
William Bompas, Madras, India.
Georgess Burgess, Stockport.
Henry Midgley, Leeds.

July 6.
Edwin Hamlyn, Plymouth.
Charles Hamlyn, Darlington.
July 7.
Mrs Atkinson, Aspatria.
July 12.
John Swift, Highfield, Sheffield.
B. Swift.
James G. Bullivant, Birmingham.
Frank Davis, Birmingham.
Are pleased to express their full and complete satisfaction at Dame
Tyson's accommodation.

Jos Twentyman, Flimby.
R.E. Twentyman, London.
Margaret Twentyman, Flimby.
Charlie Doxford, Sunderland.
Walter Campbell, Sunderland.
July 13.
W. Oxendale, Stockton on Tees.
July 18.
George Brownson, Hyde, Manchester.
Thomas Brownson.
Arthur W. Duncan, Hull, Yorkshire.

Mrs Austen, 8 Palmeria Square, Brighton.
Miss Austen.
Mr and Mrs J.H. Howard, St Witchingham, Norfolk.
Arrived on 16th in pouring rain (not unusual we believe) but had two
lovely days before leaving—enjoying the walks over Sty Head and
Black Sail immensely—Mr and Mrs Tyson made us most thoroughly
comfortable.
*In the Stone Age 4,000 years ago, there were axe making factories
on Scafell and Pike of Stickle. From these the axes were carried
down to the Cumbrian coast by way of Sty Head Pass, Windy Gap
and Ennerdale, to be used in the coastal settlements and exported to
the Isle of Man.*

July 18.
Mr Murray, Parkside Hotel, Frizington.
Mr A. Murray.

Mrs Murray.
H. Murray.
Mrs Carrick, Parkside Hotel, Frizington.
Miss Mossop, Parkside Hotel.
Miss Swan, Frizington.
Frizington is a mining village situated six miles from Whitehaven and was formerly part of the parish of Arlecdon. The church of St Paul, built in 1867-68, is constructed of crosslacon red sandstone in the early English Style.

July 19.
The visitors' book for this date contains some sketches [see illustration on page 55]. They are signed by:
Arthur L----Palethorpe, Gladstone Road, Liverpool.
Grace Palethorpe, Seaforth, Liverpool.
Elizabeth Palethorpe, Gladstone Road, Liverpool.
Were pleased beyond measure by the kindness and hospitality of Mrs Tyson and enjoyed themselves immensely during their short visit.

Edward Boden, Arthur Road, Brixton.
Joseph Thomson, Ashington under Lyme.
From Seatoller over Scarf Gap and Black Sail to here, weather fine until arrived here when detained by pouring rain. Accommodation good and charges moderate.
The village of Seatoller, in Borrowdale, lies at the foot of Honister Pass, which is the main route over the fells to the Vale of Buttermere. Although Seatoller was given its name, meaning 'Summer pasture of the Alder trees', by the Norse settlers in the 10th century, the first written record is not to be found until 1563.

July 20 to 22.
Walter Stocks, Eccles.
Frederick Thurgarland, Hyde.
Joseph Harrison, Hyde.
William A. Radcliffe, Stockport.
July 25.
Mr and Mrs G.F. Malcolmson, East Barnet, Herts.
We were delighted with the old farmhouse with its primitive ways and quaint furniture and especially with the kindness and really hospitable attention of Dame Tyson.

H. Hinkleman, Bradford.
C. Nicholson, Leeds.
S.R. Jackson, Leeds.
From Buttermere over Scarf Gap and Black Sail Passes, fine weather, very rough road.
Scarf or Scarth Gap, the pass from Buttermere to Ennerdale, runs between High Crag and The Haystacks down into the eastern end of

23

the Ennerdale valley. From there Black Sail Pass climbs between Pillar mountain and Kirk Fell and thence via the Mosedale Beck down to Wasdale Head.

July 26.
William T. Wardell, Pendleton, Manchester.
John H. Sargent, Swinton, Manchester.
J. Hadfield, Worseley, Manchester.
From Buttermere over Scarf Gap and Black Sail to Wastwater.
Weather very fine. Hostess very kind.

July 27.
Thomas Arthur Johnson, The Hermitage, Frodsham, Cheshire.
Arthur Wills, Wylde Green, Birmingham.
R.S. Benson, Rugby.
J.W. Wilson, Rugby.
A.C. Beeton, Rugby.
Rev. C.T. Arnolds, Rugby.

July 28.
M.S. Bowman, Manchester.
E.S. Parrott, Oxford.
W.H. Tarrant Jnr, Witney, Oxon.
July 30.
J.A. MacLean L.A., Edinburgh.
F.W.C. Maclean.
J.H. Acheson, Chester.
A. Maitland Wood, Liscard, Birkenhead.
August 1.
I.P. Illingham Allison, Leeds.
D.H. Battersby, Keswick.
G.H. Battersby, Repton.
R. Scriven, Dublin.
Leathes Prior, Norwich.
Leonard Bollingbroke, Norwich.
W.A. Watts, Manchester.
I.G. MacMahon, Manchester.
H. Stear, Saffron Walden.

Thomas Williams, 16 Windsor Street, Liverpool.
W.S. Blundell, 103 Great George Street, Liverpool.
James Priddam, 29 Carter Street, Liverpool.
Samuel Robinson, 16 Windsor Street, Liverpool.
CHRIST DIED FOR SINNERS. See Romans V.
Found Mr and Mrs Tyson exceedingly kind and if ever we come this way again will be glad to stay with them, will always speak well of them at home.
August 3.
J. Gibson, Church Fenton, Yorkshire.
Mr and Mrs David C. Binnie, London.

August 4.
We arrived here yesterday afternoon after walking from Drigg and left again this morning after receiving every kindness from the hands of Mr and Mrs Tyson.
John Kennaugh, 48 Chatsworth Road, Liverpool.
Isaac Marsh Jnr., London Road, Liverpool.
Edward Kennaugh, Whitehaven.
William S. Kennaugh, Whitehaven.
Three and a half miles from Ravenglass, Drigg is situated on the Cumbrian coast, where the River Irt, which flows out of Wastwater, enters the sea.

August 6.
W.M. Pendlebury, Liverpool.
E. Shannon, Liverpool.
Edward Tyson, Whitehaven.
Mrs E. Tyson.
Mannix and Whellan, in 1847, said that 'Whitehaven was anciently a place of resort for shipping.' This port, situated on the West Cumbrian coast had, at the end of the 19th century, a population of over nineteen thousand, and was the largest town in the vicinity of Wasdale Head.

August 6.
Mr and Mrs Herbert Tait have spent a most enjoyable week under Mr and Mrs Tyson's kind care and attention. They leave with much regret, heartily hoping for another opportunity of visiting this delightful haven of rest.
August 7.
Cornelius Clarke, Prospect Villa, Skipton.
Owen Owen, Devonshire Place, Skipton.
Adam Smith, Skipton.
J.M. Evans, Walton Breck Road, Liverpool.
Thomas Oates, Whitehaven.
Isaac M. Collis, Whitehaven.
H.M. Ormesby, Rossall, Fleetwood.
E.T. Pease, Darlington.
Jonathan Friend, Ambleside.
Edwin Abbs, Bradford.
A. Douglas, Bradford.
The town of Ambleside is situated in the beautiful vale of Rothay, at the head of Windermere and commands a splendid view of the lake and valley. The church of St Mary, built in 1854, is well worth visiting. At the end of the north aisle lies the Wordsworth Chapel, erected as a memorial to the distinguished poet who died on April 23rd 1850.

August 10.
Ernest W. Beeton, Stoke on Trent.

Arnold Quinsey, Rock Ferry, Cheshire.
Thomas S.M--, Grange Mount, Claughton.
James. Ed. Eckaling, Walthamstow.
Alfred D. Pinchle, London.
Miss French, London.
Miss Nunes and Master H. Nunes, London.

John Wain and M. Petty left today for Keswick by Sty Head Pass, arrived via Scarff Gap and Black Sail Pass ...(*remainder is unreadable*).

Keswick, one of the brightest jewels in the Lake Distict, is an ancient market town on the River Greta, at the lower end of Derwentwater. An historical character associated with Keswick was the 'Shepherd Lord', the only surviving son of Black Clifford, sent by his mother during the Wars of the Roses to be reared in safety as a shepherd's son on Saddlebeck. When he was 30 years old, he relinquished peaceful life of a fellside shepherd to take up his title and live in the ancestral home of Barden Tower, which still stands in the Yorkshire Dales above the River Wharfe. There he spent most of his time studying, married twice, and executed competently the public duties which his position necessitated.

August 14.
Thomas Robinson, Manchester.
August 15.
Mr and Mrs Robert Ashby, Staines.
Mr Henry Carr, Carlisle.
Herbert Barringer, London.
Edmund Barringer.
William Henry Gregory, Bradford.
Jonathan Edward Wilson, Bradford.
Mr and Mrs F. Wale, Leicester.

Herbert Todd, Norwich.
Emma Todd.
Nelly King, Norwich.
E. Fielding and Misses Fielding, Rochdale.
Came here from Buttermere yesterday, a very good walk for ladies. We were very glad this was the first house we saw, as it would have been a great mistake to pass it, being comfortable and something more like home than what we have seen lately. Mrs Tyson is all that can be desired in the way of a hostess.
Just over a century ago mine host of The Fish Inn at Buttermere was a certain Mr Robinson, who was assisted by his daughter Mary, ministering to the hunger and thirst of the many visitors. De Quincey, who knew Mary, tells of the admiration that Wordsworth and Coleridge had for her.
In 1805 a distinguished stranger arrived in Keswick and entered his name in the hotel register as the Hon. Augustus Hope M.P. He

took local society by storm and in due course arrived at the Fish Inn, ostensibly to catch char or trout. There he wooed and won Mary, the beauty of Buttermere. The happy day was fixed, it arrived and the couple after the ceremony had intended to spend their honeymoon in London. Just outside Keswick the police swooped down on Augustus and arrested him on a charge of forgery, which was the least of his many crimes, Hope, whose real name was Hatfield, was hung at Carlisle. Mary returned to Buttermere and the Fish Inn. Eventually she married a farmer from Caldbeck and her grave may be seen in the churchyard there near that of John Peel of immortal memory.

August 15.
W.H. Womersley, Bradford.
Arthur Baston, Manchester.
J.A. Walker, Manchester.

Friendly advice:

Oh tourists ye who come this way
And take up lodgings here
Beware I say of Mr Pigot
He will spring on you for naught
The village Pastor he is called
But his flock he much neglects
Preferring rather to his steeple
Rich, extremely stupid people
He is, I very much fear
Too fond a great deal of his beer.
Moral, Beware of the writer!
      Beware of the dog.

August 16.
George Hastwell, Darlington.
Jon. Hastwell, Darlington.
F.R. Smith, Dublin.
Telford Smith.

J.W. Berry, Stockton on Tees.
A.W. Kindler, Stockton.
James Kindler.
All on route for Buttermerè via the Pillar Rock. Very fine morning.
August 17.
Mrs Atkinson, London.
Miss Thornbury, London.
Mr James Williams, Egremont.
Mr R.W. Guilmette, Manchester.
G.C. Guilmette.

Reflection: It is much more pleasant to vegetate in this romantic little spot, than to traverse country such as that, which lies between

Ennerdale and Wasdale, an amount of physical exertion, which I will, in future visits forgo.
Moral: Stay at home
Yours truly, G. Guilmette.

Reflection: It would give much more pleasure to tourists if the above humbug had never brought his effeminate curse to Wastdale; better far to vegetate for his holidays in a velvet armchair.
Yours truly, E...........
August 18.
H. Smith, Manchester.
W. Clarke, Manchester.
Mr and Mrs I.W. Connon, Dewsbury.

Abner Blyth, Beverley, Yorkshire.
A very homely place for visitors.

Dawson. M. Knox, Dublin.
A.I. Pritchett, Darlington.
H.D. Pritchett.
August 20.
Rhodes. K. Calvert, Leeds.
Henry Kershaw, Leeds.
Rev. E. Wilton-South, Blackheath, London.
Mrs South.
E. Eyre.
G.O. Jacob, Blackheath.
Stayed here, weather-bound for three days. Longer than we intended, but found little cause to regret the stay. Can strongly recommend Dame Tyson's house and careful attentions.

J. Barham, Carslake, Edgbaston.
J.M.------------- London.
H. Adams.
Arrived here from Keswick, very wet, and were very pleased indeed with the kind attention and the accommodation.
J.J. Hague, London.
Alan Clark, London.
August 11 to 27.
R. Pendlebury, St Johns College, Cambridge.
August 25 to 27.
Charles. J. Seaman, Stockton on Tees, has found this the most comfortable place to stay in the Lake District, so far as his experience goes.

Albert. S. Phippen.
It would be difficult to improve upon accommodation here.
August 27.
A.K. Campbell, Union Club, London.

August 24 to 29.
J.R. Morley, Outwood Lane, Horsforth, Leeds.
Mrs Morley.
H.W. Morley, Eton College, Bucks.
All very comfortable.
August 27 to 29.
G.W. Palmer, Greenwood, Bishop's Waltham.
G.C. Bower, Wadworth Hall, Doncaster.
Mrs Hannam, Doncaster.
Wm. G. Hannam.
Miss Hirst, Doncaster.
Have great pleasure in testifying to Dame Tyson's kindness and hospitality.
August 29.
J.B. Pavey, Clifton, Bristol.

The undersigned having started from Keswick, rucksack on back, at 10 a.m., reached here at 7 p.m., by way of Honister Pass, Buttermere, where we had luncheon, Scarff Gap and Black Sail Pass (a splendid path). Were delighted to find this comfortable and homely little crib. Had a rare good tea under Mrs Tyson's special supervision.
Faulkner. A. Simon, London.
Herbert. H. Bennett, London.
Honister Pass once formed part of the boundary of the Borrowdale estate acquired by the monks of Furness Abbey in 1209. At the head of the pass lie the slate quarries, which have been worked continuously since 1643.

August 29.
Rev. Robert Daunt, Newcastle upon Tyne.
John. A. Cross, Bray, Ireland.
Very much pleased with this house.
August 31.
James. D. Cooper, Highgate London.
Walked here from Dungeon Ghyll and very glad to obtain the shelter of this comfortable home and rendered more so by the obliging character of its hostess, Dame Tyson.
Dungeon Ghyll, in Great Langdale, contains the Dungeon Ghyll Force, which falls 60 feet between rocky walls and is one of the most impressive sights in the Lake District.

September 1.
Eaton Faning, London.
Sumerville Gibney, London.
Miss Ashworth, Newcastle.
Miss Smith, Ashton on Mersey.
Miss Edith Smith, Ashton on Mersey.
Mr. W. Carpenter Jnr and the Misses Carpenter, London. 2nd visit.

September 4.
H.S. Milner, (Rossall) Elton Rectory, Stockton.
G.W.L. Fernandes, Crofton Grange, Wakefield.
September 5.
C. Hughes, Manchester.
A. Hughes.
Arrived here from Keswick via Buttermere by Scarf Gap and Black Sail. Thoroughly wet on Black Sail and most hospitably received by Dame Tyson.
September 6.
George H. Paddock, Caynt on Cottage, Newport.
West Jones, Guys Hospital, London.
F.B.I. Baldwin, Guys Hospital, London.
September 7.
Joseph Collinson, Halifax.
I.W. Collinson.
J. Cass, Barnsley.
James Cass, Castleford.
I. Staffod Anderson, Leicester.
Mrs Tyson is a most entyson sort of person. Feel rather jolly.

J. Thompson Henry.
Struggled over pass, arrived here very tired.

T.E. Raven, Sherborne.
W.E. Heitland, St Johns College, Cambridge.
Rev. T.N. Debenham, London.
Master Debenham.
Misses Debenham.
Miss N. Dalton, London.
Miss Harker, Geelong, Australia.

September 10.
Lieut. B.H. Cherallin RN, H.M.S. Excellence.
Rev. J. Miles, Battersea, London S.W.
September 15.
H. Burton Buckley, Lincolns Inn, London.
A. Burton Buckley, Italy.
C.E. Leeces, Emm College, Oxford.
A.N. Leeces, Eyebury, Peterborough.

Charles Anhurst, Daniel Tyson, Merton College, Oxford (Amicie as Keswickham relictis) after ascending Dale Head (2475 ft) the view from which is magnificient, and can compare with many mountains much higher; and traversing Scarff Gap and Windy Gap from Gatesgarth to Wastdale in one hour and forty five minutes, was lucky enough to come under the roof of Dame Tyson and went away contented and amply satisfied.
Wasdale Head is a small village, lying, as its name implies, at the

head of Wasdale valley and is acknowledged as the geographical centre of Lakeland.

September 20.
Edward B. Moser, Shrewsbury.
H. Moser, Jesus College, Cambridge.
C. Slater, St Johns College, Cambridge.
F.W. Browne, Croydon.
F. Ewbank, London.
G.L. Browne, Croydon.
D. Moore, MD., Dulwich Wood.
W. Fell Woods, Forrest Hill.
W. Noel Woods, Trinity College, Cambridge.
September 24.
Lieut. ------RN.
W.P. Dickins, Lincolns Inn.
September 25.
Rec. Canon Monahan and Mrs Monahan, Dublin.
We came from Buttermere yesterday by Scarf Gap, but caught by a shower in Black Sail we reached this house at 7 p.m., considerably wet. Nothing could exceed Mrs Tyson's kind attention and refreshing care. We leave reluctantly, but forced by prudence to use this fine day for the Sty Head Pass.

September 25.
S.F. Smithson, Jesus College, Cambridge.
W. Stuart Harris, Trinity College, Cambridge.
October 3.
H.H. Galloway, Preston.
F.B. Addison, Preston.
November 1.
W.B. Ferguson, Christ Church, Oxford.
P.B. Ferguson, Manchester.
November 22.
Mr R.A. Tyson of Beacon Hill, Penrith, visited his COUSINS here for the first time and though a comparative stranger, he received a most generous welcome.

Penrith, a market town in East Cumbria, is situated in a valley near the River Eamont. The great Roman military road from York to Carlisle passed through the town. The parish church of St Andrew, rebuilt in 1720-22 with the exception of the tower, is of red sandstone. Fine chandeliers of burnished brass were presented by the Duke of Portland in 1745. On the chancel wall is a brass plate recording the visitation of the plague in 1598. Penrith Castle, dating from about 1389, was built by the 1st Earl of Westmorland. Beacon Tower which stands on the summit of Beacon Hill, 937 feet above sea level, was built in 1719 and commands a splendid view of the mountain scenery of the two sister counties of Cumberland and Westmorland which now form Cumbria.

31

1878

March 27 to April 11.
On a readingless reading party.
I.T. Christie, Exeter College, Oxford.
H.R. King   do
H.J. Tylden   do
A.S. Butler   do
April 17th and 18.
F.W. Headley, Caius College, Cambridge.
H. Moser, Jesus College, Cambridge.
April 19.
Captain Jonathan Duck, Belmont House, Liscard, Ches.
Jonathan Joyce.
Last Good Friday the above mentioned started from Ambleside for Wastwater via Dungeon Ghyll and Rossett Ghyll, but having mistaken the road, they arrived back at Dungeon Ghyll towards evening, having made a complete circumbendibus and having over- taken on the road four other tourists, who had made the same mistake. Next day Rossett Ghyll was again attempted, and after missing the road many times, ultimately scaled, but deep snow and thick impenetrable fog prevented us arriving at Wastwater. We reluctantly turned back and arrived at Dungeon Ghyll without a dry rag on us, and shivering with cold. On April 19th we attempted the same journey again and succeeded but should have miserably failed, if the fog at one time, had not opportunely lifted. We arrived at Dame Tysons in a state approaching knocked- upishness and forthwith revelled in clover. Weather as usual about as wet as can be, 9.a.m., 20th April. The sleep of the proverbial top was ours last night. Allah Akbar 'Let the bracing and cheering effects of a pouring wet morning be my excuse for this effusion'.
Jonathan Duck.
April 23.
Fred Whittle, Cleator Moor (Solicitor).
Henry Rothery, Cleaton Moor.
Arthur Whittle, Whitehaven.
The church of St John the Evangelist at Cleator Moor was conse-
crated on June 25th 1872. Built of red sandstone, it is late Norman

style. The register dates from 1869.

April 25.
Robert Leighton, Wakefield.
Edwin Harrison, Oxford.
Herbert Richards, Oxford.
P.S. Quintin, Hampstead.
William. J. Nixon, London Hospital.
May 27.
W. George and family, Bradford.
Mrs. M.B. George, Leeds.
May 28.
J.W. Jameson, Banker, Perth.
E.S. McGilchrist, Perth.
Arrived her on a lovely evening from Buttermere, with a trusty guide (without whom no-one should attempt wandering among these hills), Edward Nelson, ready to do justice to Mrs Tyson's delightful tea and ham and eggs. Delighted with the majestic scenery.
May 29.
Robert. R. Cowan, Maryport.
Edward Weddell, Maryport.
Left Maryport at 8 o'clock in the morning.
Ratie Cowan, Maryport.
Maryport, formerly a busy sea-port town on the West Cumbrian coast, saw its first shipbuilding yard opened in 1765, and in the same year a brig, 'The Sally', of 106 tons was built and launched.

May 30.
Charles. E. Franklin, Beccles, Suffolk.
June 7.
Mr Neilson, Liverpool.
Mrs Earle, Windermere.
June 10.
E. Harland, Sunderland.
Jonathan Parker, Sunderland.
D. Ranken, Sunderland.
I. Ranken.
I. Grubb, Sunderland.
I. Cobb, Sunderland.
R. Wilson, Sunderland.
Arrived well wet, but were soon made comfortable.

John James and Bryan Barnard, spent three days here in June 1878, found food and lodgings, and all things most satisfactory.
W.T. Marples, Sharrow, Sheffield.
Master. W.S. Marples.
Master. E.O. Marples.
Most clean, comfortable and satisfactory.

June 11.
Aldington, London.
M.J. Fuller, London.
June 11 to 13.
Charles Campbell, Bradford.
June 11.
Daniel Tyson Satterthwaite.
Mrs Andrew Herbert.
Mr Joseph Satterthwaite.
Mr Thomas Benn.
Miss Rachael Satterthwaite.
Miss Elizabeth Barwise.
Miss Sarah Dixon.
Miss Eleanor Satterthwaite.
We all enjoyed our ham and eggs immensely and we thank Mrs Tyson for her kindness and good attention.
June 13 to 14.
J.S. Jowett, Brighouse.
John Lord Jnr. do.
Joseph Exelby, do
Colonel Lindsay, Edinburgh.
Miss Rennie,   do
Thomas Bolton, Moor Court, Staffs.
T.A. Colfox, Bridport.
Very sorry not to have allowed time for a longer stay.
June 14.
H.A. Hentsch, Battersea.
A.W. Cox, Clapham.
H. Newbery, Camberwell.
John W. Holford, Southport.
Mrs J.W. Holford,   do
Miss Bramall,   do
Miss M.E. Bramall, do
Miss Holford, Birkdale.
June 15.
Robert. J. West, Penge, London.
Charles Percy West, Crosby, Liverpool.
A wish ....
May health and happiness
Peace and prosperity
Attend you through life.
June 18.
Walter Lewis, Blackburn.
Harry Bragg, Blackburn.
Left Buttermere at 11.30 a.m., came by Scale Force, Red Pike, High Sty, Scarf Gap and Black Sail Passes. Have enjoyed their meals and are perfectly satisfied with the kind treatment they have received.

June 20.
Rev. Arthur J. Smith, Levens Parsonage, Milnthorpe.
Rev. R. Keightly-Smith, Bridekirk, Cockermouth.
William Wordsworth was born at Cockermouth on April 7th, 1770.
His father, John, was attorney-at-law at Cockermouth and agent for
Sir James Lowther, afterwards the Earl of Lonsdale. William's
childhood was spent at Cockermouth and with his mother's family,
the Cooksons of Penrith.

June 21.
G. Boddington-Smith, 10 Holford S, London.
Found Dame Tyson most kind and attentive — one of the good old
school.

Rowland Smith, Chief Officer, 'Carry Vernon'.
Arrived by Black Sail from Buttermere and left for Ambleside
over Scafell Pike next morning, much pleased with Dame Tyson's
gooseberry cake, and I am -------
The best way to enjoy Ambleside is to climb up the twisting road
which crosses Stock Ghyll and savour the succession of views which
open up as you climb.

June 22.
J.M. Barber, Manchester.
J.N. Sutcliffe, Bacup.
Joseph Hale, Walshaw, Dewsbury.
Barometer 30.3 at sea level (rising), splendid prospect promising for
Scafell.
There is nothing in the Lake District over 3,000 feet outside the
Helvellyn, Skiddaw, Scafell triangle.

June 23.
Josiah Hosking, Liverpool.
Edgar Hosking,   do

F.W. Taylor, Great Bardfield, Essex.
G.I. Harrison, Liverpool.
Joseph. J. Swinborn, Bayswater, London.
June 21 from ...
The Rev W.J. Margetts, and the Rev Henry Moody, both from
Leeds, cannot speak too highly of Dame Tyson's homely hospitality.
June 26.
Rev. Isaac Robinson, St. John the Evangelist, Holborn.
Mrs Robinson.

John. W. Holford, Southport.
Mrs Holford.
Miss Carrie Holford.
Miss Bramall and Miss M.E. Bramall.
second visit.

July 4.
Pheobe E. Batt, Milnthorpe.
Emily Stringer, Bristol.
Elizabeth Stringer, Bristol.
July 10.
John Lund.
Mrs Lund, Sidney Sussex College, Cambridge.
Arrived here at 7.15 p.m. over Black Sail from Buttermere (having reached the last named spot at 3 p.m. from Thirlmere via Rosthwaite) and have much pleasure in testifying to the comfort and cleanliness of this welcome resting place.
Thirlmere lies beside the familiar and continuously beautiful road from the delightful village of Grasmere to Keswick. The first view of Thirlmere which greets the visitor is from the downward winding road from the pass of Dunmail Raise, deep channelled between the rugged wall of Armboth Crags and the northern shoulders of Helvellyn, with Skiddaw in the distance.

July 12.
John Hendrie, Glasgow and Ayr.
Peter Paterson, Victoria Park, Ayr.
Rev Edward Thornton, Whitburn, Sunderland.
Thomas H. Scott, Cleadon, Sunderland.
From Keswick.
July 13.
N. Ritson, Carlisle.
Carlisle, the ancient border town, is also capital of the county of Cumbria. It was here in 1568 that Mary, Queen of Scots, who had fled from her own subjects, arrived from Workington, where she had landed, only to find herself made a prisoner in Carlisle Castle.

July 14.
William Thompson, Burnley.
J.A. Waddington, Burnley.
James Lancaster,   do
Mrs Lancaster,   do
William Witham,   do

H.R. King, Exeter College, Oxford.
W. Trevor, Balliol College, Oxford.
H.H. Evans, Oriel College, Oxford.
A.N. Scott, Exeter College, Oxford.

E. and S.J. Tyson, Beacon Hill, Penrith, came here on the 10th July and enjoyed their visit very much. They came via Keswick and Seathwaite over the Sty Head Pass and received a hearty welcome from their kind and hospitable COUSINS.
Seathwaite which stands on the River Derwent had in the 19th century a plumbago mine.

36

July 14.
George Ames, Sible Hedingham, Essex.
N.H. Coles, Castle Hedingham, Essex.
Having missed our way and gone over Great Gable instead of Black Sail and having to retrace our steps, we reached here at 11 p.m. Mr Tyson had gone to bed, but at the first knock Mr Tyson came down and admitted us, strangers as we were, most kindly. We shall always remember our hearty welcome.

A route gaining in popularity by the latter years of the 19th century for the ascent of Great Gable, was by striking across the Wasdale face from Kern Knotts, near Sty Head, along the climber's path below the Napes Ridges, then upwards just before the Sphinx Ridge.

July 16.
Rev. J. Stroud, South Perrot Rectory, Dorset.
July 18.
R. Knowles, Bradford.
Nicholas Brown, Bradford.
S. Eadie, St Johns Terrace, Jarrow on Tyne.
M.F. Harmer, St Johns Terrace, Jarrow.
M. Muriel, Whitehaven.
July 24.
A.D. Stallard, Trinity College, Cambridge.
R.B. Walmsley, Trinity College.
E.J. Nanson, Trinity College, Cambridge and Carlisle.
G.H. Gray, Jesus College, Cambridge and Carlisle.
George Edgecombe, Waterloo.
A. Vertice, Thornville, Teddington.
G.G. Vertice.
July 25.
Edmund S. Taylor, I.S.R., London.
Robert Gray Jrn, I.S.R., London.
July 26.
Leonard Bradley, Brixton.
William Bradley.
From Keswick via Buttermere, Scarf Gap, Black Sail to Coniston by Scafell Pike.
July 27.
G.B.I. Mason.
Mrs. G.B.I. Mason.
On the way to Coniston.

A most favourite hunting ground for climbers is within one hour's walk of Coniston. It is part of the range of hills that includes Wetherlam and Coniston Old Man [2, 638 feet]. From Coniston Old Man looking westward you can see the summit of Doe Crag some 900 feet above the lake itself.

July 31.
Herbert Wills Kitson, London.

From Rosthwaite via Buttermere, Scarf Gap and Black Sail. Stayed one day and ascended Scafell, was made thoroughly comfortable by the kindness of Mr and Mrs Tyson and regret I cannot remain longer.

Until motor coaches were introduced after the 1914-18 War, a horse coach would run from Keswick to Rosthwaite three times a day in the summer. A four-horse coach carried a total of 21 passengers.

July 31.
Marshall Armstrong, Irton.
Thomas Armstrong, Shipley, Yorkshire.
Samuel Tyson, Croft Cottage, Santon, Irton.
Edward Thornycroft, Manchester.
John Seddon, Manchester.
George Edward Thornton, Keighley.
John Judson, Draper, Keighley.

On the road and through
All intent on getting good
All from Keswick by Rosthwaite
Honister Crag to Buttermere and Crummock
Over Black Sail to Wastwater.
On the west side from Crummock Water in a chasm on one side of Red Pike is a cascade known as Scale Force. This is the loftiest waterfall in the whole of the Lake District having a descent of 180 feet.

August 2.
Charlotte Hanbury, Wellington, Somerset.
Bessis Hanbury, Stoke Newington.
Stayed here this two nights, much enjoying the comforts and the kindness in this pleasant home.

John. F. Haworth, Manchester.
J.F. Pearson,   do
Most pleased with the attention—don't miss the waterfall.

Joseph James Tyson, Arnold Cottage, East Amhurst Rd., Hackney, London.
Hannah Mary Watson, Great Clifton, Workington.
Workington has a long history. As far back as 1202, salmon fishing facilities were granted to the monks of Holme Cultram Abbey, and their famous fisheries continued until 1863. It was here at Workington on May 16th, 1568, that Mary, Queen of Scots came to seek asylum from Queen Elizabeth.

August 2.
Thomas Williams, Liverpool.
W.S. Blundell.
R. Smith.

John McKenzie.
J. Priddon.
S. Robinson.
Thomas Williams.
Very comfortable at Mrs Tyson's house and will stay here when in
these parts again. 'Behold the Lamb of God'.
August 4.
Rev. C.A. Lowry, Carlisle.
C. Lowry, C.C.C., Oxford.
A.H. Stanton, Oxford.

Obadiah Richardson.

The following gentlemen spent a most agreeable day at Wastdale-
head, after making a tour of the highest Mountain in England, visit-
ing and attending Service in the smallest church in England, calling
upon the celebrated Will Ritson (noted for his Foxhounds) and
enjoying a most hearty repast at Mr and Mrs Tysons, left for Gosforth
at 2.30 on the fourth August 1878.
Thomas Watson, Barrow in Furness.
N. Hardy.
W.A. Maxwell.
I. Smith.
W.P. Armstrong, Ireland.
Wm. Watson, Barrow in Furness.

John Hastings, Corpus Christi, Oxford.
C.A. Vansittart, Corpus Christie, Oxford.
H.G.M. Conybeare, Ingatestone, Essex.
Mr and Mrs George Sparrow.
Miss Nannie Sparrow.
Miss Browne, Wexford.
C.C. White, 22 Lowther Street, Whitehaven.
From Buttermere over the two passes en route to Keswick via Sty
Head. Well received by Mr and Mrs Tyson.
*The Lakes poet Coleridge with his family came to live at Greta Hall,
near Keswick, overlooking Derwentwater in July 1810. His last
great poem 'Ode to Dejection' appeared on Wordsworth's wedding
day as a compliment to the great Cumbrian poet.*

August 4.
Mr. G. Williamson and C.N. Taylor, Whitehaven, came up
Ennerdale Lake in a boat past --------- Tarn, up Buttermere, over
Honister to Keswick, stayed over night, then from Keswick down the
water by boat, through Borrowdale over the Sty Head Pass and were
received by Mrs Tyson in grand style.
August 5.
The Misses Bernard, Clifton.
Miss Marshall, Hampstead.

Miss A.M. Ware, Clifton.

I.H. Bernard, Clifton College.

F. Spencer Bell, Fow Park, Derwentwater.

The 1st Earl of Derwentwater was created by James II in 1688. His son who succeeded to the title in 1705 was executed on February 24th, 1716, on Tower Hill, for playing a leading part in the Jacobite rebellion.

August 6.

Alfred J. Faulding and lady, London.

J.W.B. Mason and Miss Marsh, London.

Alfred. H. White, London. N.W.

T. Gurnell Parry, Liverpool.

James I. Gledsdale, Liverpool.

August 7.

William Henry Longmaid, Kendal.

John William Jones, London.

A. Nicholson, Maryport.

Some of the punishable offences included in the Maryport Improvement and Harbour Act of 1866 included playing pitch and toss; football; shuttlecock; tipcat; trundling hoops; running races; throwing snowballs or bathing in forbidden places. The town had a strict law against brothel keepers, these persons being liable to heavy fines or imprisonment.

August 8.

James Tyson, Wavertree, Liverpool.

Isaac Hipkin, Whitehaven.

Edward Proctor, Newcastle.

S.J. Taylor, Newcastle.

N.A. Murray, Edinburgh.

Charles Robertson, Edinburgh.

Rev. A.E. Robinson, Trinity College, Cambridge.

W. Welsh, Altringham.

August 9.

Henry Briggs, South Shields.

T.D. Hailes,

George Hudson,

John. W. Hirley, all of South Shields.

August 10.

J.R. Brown, Carlisle.

And two others came from Coniston by Dungeon Ghyll over the Pike and down Lingmell Ghyll to Mrs Tysons of Wasdale Head.

Passing over the head of a stream called Piers Ghyll, you can see the summit of Lingmell [2,649 feet].

August 10.

Edwin. J. Derrington, Birmingham.

From Buttermere to Ennerdale, from Ennerdale over Windy Gap

between Pillar and Steeple to Wastdale Head. Moral, ye who read this, 'don't go over Windy Gap'.
Joseph Wilson, Free Press Officer, Spalding.
Charles Vivian, Camberwell, London.
Pearce Herrington, Birmingham.
Rev. Thomas Maylor, Sandbach, Cheshire.
August 11.
Eustace Carey, Widnes.
John. R. Pickard, Kirkby Lonsdale.
F.E. Shepherd, Holme.
Walter Shepherd, Dundee.

H.L. Mouk, India.
J.A. Lowin, Coopers Hill, Surrey.
August 12.
R. Hindle, Ulverston.
E.A. Hindle,   do

I. Singleton, Ulverston.
B.F. Singleton,   do
O for mountains, lakes, valleys, woods, waters, and meadows,
Canny auld Cumberland — them are still.
August 13.
Joshua O'Brien, Belfast.
Charles James Abbatt, Bolton.
Frederick. W. Jackson,   do
Frederic Wright,   do
Benjamin. F. O'Brien, Bolton.
I. Owden O'Brien, Liverpool.
August 14.
Edwin Gledhill, Lindley, Huddersfield.
William Henry Brook, Manchester.
H. Threlfall, York.
F.A. Hall, York.

Mrs Musgrave and family, Wasdale Hall.
Misses Lazonby, Didsbury Manchester.
August 15.
Joseph Vevers, Leeds.
Rhodes K. Calvert, Leeds.

J.F. Richards, Teddington.
R.D. Bishop, Kensington.
Food and attention very good.

H.J. Roby, Pendleton.
A.G. Roby, Pendleton.

H.G. Gibson, Wadham College, Oxford.

41

Miss Trust, London.

Miss Noverre, Norwich.

Have spent two days most agreeably in this delightful place and thank Dame Tyson for her very great kindness and attention.

William. J. Harding, Sidney Sussex College, Cambridge.

I. Bain Fowler, Brecon.

W.W. Fowler, Lincoln College, Oxford.

Mr and Mrs Basil Martineau, Barnsbury, London.

Very much pleased with house, food and Mrs Tyson's attention.

Arthur Chandler, Putney.

Made very comfortable and much pleased.

August 19.

Walter Chambers, Liverpool.

John. W. Briggs, Nottingham.

James Molineux, Carlisle, Aug 10-18.

Lieut Colonel Rolandson and party were recipients of Mrs Tyson's hospitality and were most gratified with the attention and comfort obtained.

August 20.

Mr and Mrs David Grimshaw, from Leeds.

Miss S.C. Armytas, Leeds.

Well treated.

August 21.

N.E. Allman, Hull.

Edwin Fenton, Hull.

August 22.

Rev. T.E. Hankins on Cox.

Rev. E.F.E. Hankinson.

Clara Dryden, Putney.

A.E. Dryden, Putney.

Very comfortably and pleasantly entertained.

August 23.

George Bernard, Highfield, Sheffield.

Austin. W. Bernard.

Victor Smith.

Travers Smith.

Miss Sibbett and Miss H.A. Sibbett; R. Sibbett; S. Sibbett of York.

R. Roundthwaite, London; in passing from Buttermere to this house missed the path in Ennerdale Valley and reached here over the mountains between Great Gable and Kirk Fell at 10 p.m. Very hospitably treated.

The River Liza feeds Ennerdale Lake from the eastern end. It has its source on Great Gable [2,949 feet].

August 23.
I.N. Greenwood, Coventry.
I.F. Greenwood, Coventry.
F.I. Greenwood, Coventry.
Very comfortable.
August 24.
James Harper,
Andrew Dalziel, were made exceedingly comfortable here by Mrs
Tyson, Wasdale Head.

Frances. E. Wilson, Southport.
Eustace. Frith, Reigate.
Percy George Shadbolt.
L.P. Shadbolt.
Could not wish for better quarters.
*It is often said that anyone who believes he is a climber would
never dream of leaving Wasdale without climbing Great Gable.
When visiting Wasdale Head do visit the church. It is only 42 feet
long and 16 feet wide and possesses just three windows and eight
pews, with a tiny bell tower.*

August 26.
Rochfort Davies, Chelsea, London.
Comfortable.

Dixon. C. Davies, Sydenham, London.

August 28.
Gildart Jackson, Leith.
Mrs Jackson.
W.G. Jackson.
C.R. Foster, Leith.
Walked from Buttermere to top of Great Gable and down to
Wasdale Head via Sty Head Pass. Returned next day via Black Sail
and Scarf Gap Passes. Found most comfortable quarters at Mrs
Tyson's.
*Black Sail Pass [1,600 feet] is the starting point for the ascent of
both Steeple and Pillar, two of the most well-known climbs in the
Lake District.*

September 9.
Thomas Pyke, South Shields.
John. T. Harvey, Nottingham.
W.G.C. Rayne, Nottingham.
L. Gethring, Newport. Mons.
September 10.
H.G.E. Green, St Johns Wakefield, and A.H. Smith, Skelwith
Bridge, walked from Skelwith Bridge and enjoyed it very much.

C.W. James, Barrock Park, Cumberland; J.A. Hanham, Magdalen College, Oxford.

The Skelwith Bridge area was once noted for smugglers and moonshiners. The most notorious moonshiner in the Lake District was Lanty Slee who lived between Skelwith Bridge and Coniston. He had a number of stills concealed about the neighbouring fells to outwit the authorities. He died aged 78 years in 1878 at Greenbank Farm.

September 10.
Stephen Donne, Oswestry.
Rev. I.M. Donne, Northampton.
Spent a very pleasant evening and were made most comfortable by Dame Tyson.
Alfred J.P. Shepherd, Queen's College, Oxford.
C.S. Shepherd, Blackheath.
September 13.
W.H. Mitchell, Bradford.
F. Mitchell, Bradford.
H. Mitchell, Bradford.
G.H. Muller, Bradford.

E.S. Milnes Walton, Derbyshire.
W. Allan Angell, Manchester.
Edwin Holt, Manchester.
August 29 to September 18.
R. Pendlebury, St Johns College, Cambridge.

Jonathan. H. and C. Leonard Terry, Hadley, Herts.
W.F. Turner, Welbeck Street, London.
B.B. Turner, Junior, The Lawn, Tulse Hill, London.
September 17 to 20.
Arthur. T. Wills, Wylde Green, Birmingham.
A.W. Wills,   do
Harry Rowe, London.

William Exeley, Shipley, Yorkshire.
Robert. E. Weatherhead, Bingley, Yorks.
September 21.
H. Strobach, Bedford St, Liverpool.
E. Ludeke. BA., Bedford Street, Liverpool.
October 2.
Rev. P.R. Robin, Woodchurch Rectory.
Mrs Robin, Woodchurch Rectory.
The Misses Robin.
October 3.
Mr and Mrs Robinson, Lyn Hales, Herefordshire.
Mr and Mrs George Barrow, Birmingham.
Arthur. M. Bramall, London.
October 8.
Miss Braithwaite, Hall Flatt, Seaton.

44

Miss Clarke, Low Mill House.
Miss C. Hartley, Egremont.
Miss Holliday, Egremont.
G. Clarke, Egremont.
N. Salmon, Thornflatt, Drigg.

Egremont, an ancient market town, stands on the River Ehen. The church of St. Mary was originally a Norman structure erected about 1130. A new church was built on the site in 1881 in the Early English style.

October 8.
Miss Braithwaite, Hall Flatt, Santon.
Miss Clarke, Low Mill House.
Miss Hartley, Egremont.
Miss Holliday, do
G. Clarke, do
N. Salmon, Thornflatt, Drigg.
October 11.
H.S. Williams, Liverpool.
A.C. Abraham, Liverpool.
Left Scafell Hotel, Rosthwaite at 10.30. After fording the river in several places up to their knees, arrived at the Fish, Buttermere at 2 p.m. Having lunched, they started for Wasdale Head at 2.45 and having crossed Scarf Gap and arrived at the top of Black Sail, darkness set in and they were obliged to make the rest of the way in heavy rain, down the pass; following the stream, and climbing from rock to rock and over numberless walls to this place (arrived 7.15). They would strongly recommend tourists not to leave Buttermere for this place later than 1.30 in bad weather at this time of the year. They may add, that on arriving here, they met with a very hospitable reception from Dame Tyson and were supplied with an excellent tea, which was most acceptable.
A.C.A.
H.S.W.

Advice to those about to walk from Buttermere here — don't.

F. Wilson (Coledale), arrived here October 14th after a pleasant three hours walk from Buttermere. Was comfortably received by Dame Tyson.
October 18.
Henry Joseph Hall, Kensington.

1879

March 21.
Charles A. Scott (Uppingham), Victoria Park, Manchester.
From Keswick via Buttermere, Scarf Gap and Black Sail Passes.
March 29 to April 12.
I. M. King, Windermere.
April 2.
Claude Wilson, Edinburgh.
Francis E. Wilson, Southport.
April 1 to 4.
H. Moser, Jesus College, Cambridge.
April 10.
B. Hainsworth, Rossall.
H. M. Ormesby.
C. B. Ogden.
Thomas Mahir.
April 11 to 13.
N. Woolley.
C. Hopkinson.
A. Hopkinson.
April 14.
E. C. Kendall, Liverpool.
J. W. H. Thorp, Macclesfield, Cheshire.
April 10 to 14.
Mr and Mrs I. Dewhurst Milne, Cheadle, Manchester.
March 27 to April 14.
H. R. King, Exeter College, Oxford.
F. R. Meuricoffre, Naples, and Trinity Coll, Cambridge.
A. S. Butler, South Hill, Park Rd, Liverpool.
April 14.
R. Adamson, Queens College, Manchester.
A. S. Wilkins, Queens College, Manchester.
From Grasmere by Dungeon Ghyll and Rossett Pass here.
The rushbearing festival survives still at Grasmere and takes place
on the Saturday nearest to St Oswald's Day, August 5th. Children
bring their bearings to the churchyard wall and, after walking

46

through the village, 'pass to the wide church door', charged with the offerings that their fathers bore. After a short service the bearings are left in the church.

April 16.
Stephen ---, Fairfield, Manchester.
April 22 to 23.
T. W. Wilson, Sherborne, Dorset.
T. E. Raven, Dorset.
May 4 to 5.
F. F. Gordon, London
A. Macintosh, London.
May 16.
J. T. Johnston, West Derby, Liverpool.
May 28.
R. R. Cowan, Maryport.
Pat Cowan.
June 1.
George Olwen, High Broughton, Manchester.
Horace Wyles,   do
Alfred Smith, Lower Broughton.
June 1 to 2.
Can entirely endorse the many testimonials as to the kindness and hospitality of Mrs Tyson.
Robert Melross, Glasgow.
Miss R. Taylor, Parton.
June 2 to 3.
Frank E. Slingsby, Carleton, Skipton.
William Cecil Slingsby,   do
June 3.
O traveller rest at Mrs Tysons
Her ham is good, the eggs are nice uns
When I was here our numbers plenty,
Came to exactly two and twenty.
The old hens laid till sore distrest,
For milk the cows did all their best.
Our hostess kind we found and able,
As she should be, who owns Great Gable.
H. A. Inch, London.
John Glover, Darlington.
M. Henderson, Darlington.

Luke S. Walmsley, Blackburn.
H. Lodge, Blackburn.
Thomas Hand, Blackburn.
Herbert Higson, Blackburn.

S. Taylor Gill, Sheffield.
J. Barton, Sheffield.

W. B. Jackson, Sheffield.

John K. Bolton, Preston.
John Forshaw, Preston.
From Coniston over Burnmoor to Buttermere over Pillar.
On Burnmoor above Eskdale there are Bronze Age burial places.

June 3.
Thomas K. Catchpool, Leicester.
From Borrowdale by Buttermere and Ennerdale.
*Earliest known Christian settlements in Borrowdale date from about
1200, when the valley passed into the hands of two famous abbeys,
Fountains and Furness.*

June 4.
Samuel Tyson, Santon.
Mrs Tyson, London.
Miss Forbes, London.
J. M. Tyson, London.
T. B. Tyson, London.
The last three, after ascending Scafell, returned to Mrs Tysons and
all enjoyed a most comfortable bed.

June 5.
I. B. Anderson, Leicester.
From Rosthwaite by Buttermere and Ennerdale. The previous day
Pillar Mountain and Rock.

June 6.
James Etchells, Newton Heath, Manchester.
A. N. Lawton, Manchester.

June 9.
Frank Ashwell, Nottingham.
Henry Wilson, London.
Edward Burgess, London.

June 11.
Richard Ashby, Oldham.

James Snape, Manningham, Bradford.
June 12th left for Buttermere.
*One of the easiest walks from Buttermere to Ennerdale goes up Sour
Milk Ghyll past Bleaberry Tarn to the top of Red Pike, a steep
descent to the valley below and then to Ennerdale.*

June 14.
C. Herbert, Lee, Kent.
W. F. Sinclair, Calcutta.

June 18.
From Coniston by Fellfoot, Dungeon Ghyll, Rosset Ghyll, Sty Head
Pass. Had a most enjoyable bed and started next morning for Scafell
Pikes.

Row Farm, Wasdale Head, the base for many of Lakeland's pioneer rock-climbing exploits during the latter part of the 19th century when it was a guest-house run by Thomas and Mary Ann Tyson. The visitors' books kept during much of this period form the basis of the present work. Great Gable broods almost menacingly above the farm. (Tom Parker).

Above: Sphinx Rock, Great Gable, with the Wasdale valley lying far below. (A.F.Kersting)

Opposite:- Top, left: Walter Parry Haskett-Smith, the 'father of English rock-climbing', who entered some fascinating and detailed descriptions of pioneer climbs in the Row Farm visitors' books.

Top right: This poor-quality photograph, included for its great historical interest, shows J. W. Robinson of Whinfell Hall, Lorton, leading a climb on Scafell Pinnacle. Robinson, whose name also frequently appears in the visitors' books, was one of the greatest of Lakeland's early climbers.

Bottom: Pillar Rock, showing in the right foreground Robinson's Cairn, built on Easter Saturday 1908 under the direction of W. P. Haskett-Smith as a memorial to J.W.Robinson.

Above: R. J. Birkett and C. R. Wilson climbing Kern Knotts, Great Gable.
Opposite: A climber on the same mountain's Arrowhead route. (Tom Parker).

The Wastwater Hotel (top) now has as its annexe the Huntsman Inn, founded by the legendary Will Ritson who described Wasdale as containing 'the highest mountain, the deepest lake, the smallest church and the biggest liar' in England. Ritson is buried at Wasdale church (bottom); his gravestone is in the foreground with its apex pointing to the centre window.

These two sketches embellish the entries in the visitors' books for July 19th, 1877.

A magnificent panorama of Wasdale as seen from the top of the screes above Wastwater
The three peaks conspicuous in the background are, from left to right, Yewbarrow, Kirk
Fell and Great Gable. (William F. Meadows).

Alfred Reman, Hackney, London.
Fellfoot lies in Little Langdale above Little Langdale Tarn, about one mile up the road to Wrynose. Behind an old farmhouse there is a terraced mound, which some believe to be a Viking Parliament-Mount.

June 19.
From Keswick via Sty Head Pass — to Piers Ghyll — thence to summit of Great Gable — over Black Sail and Scarf Gap to Honister and Buttermere — Scale Force.
J. Elliot, Wolverhampton.
Henry Haden Kenrick, Wolverhampton.

From Keswick Sty Head Pass, Piers Ghyll up Great Gable, Wastwater Lake, back by Black Sail, Honister Pass etc.
Alfred Cooke, Durham.

Mr and Mrs George O. Joy, Leeds.
June 21.
From Grange over Sty Head Pass in pouring rain. Found a haven of rest at Mrs Tysons. We are loth to depart but an anxious landlady awaits us; ten more miles in the rain.
Miss Mary Taylor, London.
Lydia Whitehead, London.
Margaret Taylor, London.
Janet Taylor, London.
When the Borrowdale area came under the jurisdiction of Furness Abbey, monks from there came to live in Grange to look after the Abbey's interests. Some of the buildings they used are still inhabited. The granary was converted into three houses.

June 25.
Louis Thielebeule, Birkenhead.
F. W. Thielebeule, Jnr.
From Keswick by Buttermere over Scarf Gap and Black Sail. Splendid weather all day.
June 26.
Frank Johnson, York.
Charles I. Milne, Newcastle upon Tyne.
Arrived here from Rosthwaite over Sty Head Pass. Rained hard all the way. Found very comfortable quarters here.
Near to the village of Rosthwaite is the Bowder Stone. Estimated to weigh almost 2,000 tons, it is roughly 30 feet high and 60 feet long. Probably the largest perfectly poised rock in the world, it is a major tourist attraction.

June 29.
W. M. Pendlebury, Liverpool.
R. Pendlebury, St Johns College, Cambridge.

Josiah Hoskins, Liverpool.
E. E. Dufton, Liverpool.
June 30.
J. E. Rose, North Shields.
Mr and Mrs H. Petty, Hull.
Left 31st for Dungeon Ghyll, via Rosset Gill. Accommodation very comfortable indeed.
Rosset Gill in Great Langdale leads up to Hanging Knott, Angle Tarn and Esk Hause.

June 30.
E. Little.
T. Jenkinson.
I. G. Steele.
From Ennerdale to Grasmere.
July 2.
W. Hemingway Shaw, Derby.
A. Mathew Butt, Chester.
John T. Barker, Leeds.
J. Newman Barker, London.
William Edward Barker, Louth.

C. E. Cairnes, Trinity College, Dublin.
William H. Windle, Trinity College, Dublin.
July 3.
Mrs Banks, Liverpool.
Spent a very pleasant week, the only drawback wet weather.
July 8.
John H. Holford, Southport.
Mrs Holford, Southport.
Miss Bramall,   do
Mary E. Bramall, Southport.
Annie Johnson, Aughton, Ormskirk.
Caroline C. Holford, Birkdale Park, Southport.
3rd visit.

E. Woolley, Burbage, Buxton.
R. Woolley, Collingham, Newark.
July 11.
Ambrose B. Walford, Trinity Hall, Cambridge.
Selwyn Puckle, Trinity Hall, Cambridge.
Came over Scafell from Borrowdale and were most hospitably received by Mrs Tyson.

J. Foster-Elliott, University College, Durham and Ashford, Kent.
Lieut. Col. Campbell, Charing, Herts.

Dr. A. H. Carmichael thanks Mr and Mrs Tyson very much for great kindness and attention during a very wet day. Liverpool.

Wasdale Head clergymen and schoolmasters had the privilege of using their whittles at the tables of their parishioners, by way of helping out their scanty stipend. This custom prevailed until 1864 and ceased with the death of the schoolmaster. Where there were very few children it was necessary to support the schoolmaster in this manner: if a family sent four children to the Wasdale Head school, the master stayed four weeks at their home.

July 14.
Mrs Dodgson, Great Crosby, Liverpool.
Miss Harrison.
Miss Dodgson.
Miss Emily Dodgson.
Miss Ellen Higson
Arthur Ch------ all of Liverpool.
July 17.
D. Johnstone, Westbourne Grove, Bayswater, London.
J. Ivison, Preston.
T. Bullough, Preston.
R. F. Brown, Cockermouth.
J. Cook, Cockermouth.
Came from Buttermere via Scarf Gap and Black Sail Pass, visited Barnards Cairn. Most comfortable and reasonable quarters at Fish Hotel, Buttermere.

Robert Salinger, St Peters Park, London.
Arthur I. Wright, Cambria Terrace, Leeds.
George W. Atkinson, Hunslet, Leeds.
July 18.
Henry O'Hannah, Dublin.
Maria Wigham,   do
Leonard Wigham, Dublin.
Arnold Wigham,   do
Alfred Peile, Stainburn House, Workington.
A. Ernest Peile,   do
From Kirkgate, Loweswater, via Scarf Gap and Black Sail, en route to Eskdale.
Seven miles from Cockermouth, Loweswater is the northernmost of three lakes which lie across this part of the county, the others being Crummock and Buttermere.

July 18.
Gerard Moore Mason, Corpus Christi College, Cambridge.
Harry W. Russell, Watford.

Here the weary may find rest,
And (if wet) in a pair of Mr Tyson's breeches be dressed
That is, if of the masculine Gender
If of the femine, Mrs Tyson will attend her.

W. T. Sherwood.

E. Jones.

J. Brown.

R. Scott.

July 21.

To Buttermere and Crummock
With an empty stomach
Came Tommy Greenall;
Who with his friend James Jackson
Both with their packs on
Proceeded to Wasdale Head,
By Scarf Gap and Black Sail,
Not as fast as the Scotch Mail.
They came into Wasdale
At six o'clock.
They found Mrs Tyson
Who is such a nice un
(Observe the expression
And grammar too).

The head of Crummock lies about a mile south of Loweswater. On one side of the lake rocks rise from the water's edge to the heights of Melbreak (1,676 feet) and Scale Knott (1,000 feet), while the road runs along the other edge of the lake.

July 22.

Rev. T. H. Grose, Queens College, Oxford.	
B. R. Wise,	do
W. N. Wilson,	do
J. F. Longrigg,	do

July 23.

Frederick Leach.

Everard Hopkins, Oak Hill, Hampstead.

From Buttermere en route to Langdale.

John Tyson, London.

J. T. Tyson, London.

T. Green, London.

V. Green, London.

Young people in the country, particularly in Buttermere, used to assemble on a winter evening and subscribe a few pence each to buy treacle for making taffy and to enjoy the fun of slyly besmearing each other's faces. When there used to be a 'Taffy Join' the custom was to ask a lot of young men and women. They all paid so much each for the treacle and sugar — hence the name.

July 24.

Claud Wilson, Edinburgh.

Frank Wilson, Southport.

Rev. C. Ward, Newton le Willows.

Rev. S. Trundle, York.

Left Whitehaven by rail, walked from Cleator Moor to Ennerdale, thence by Vale of Liza and Scarf Gap to Wasdale Head. Thoroughly appreciated Dame Tyson's hospitality.
William Gladstone, Glasgow University.
William Lyon, Ayr, NB.

J. Bourne Eccleston, Hertford College, Oxford.
Everything nice here except the weather.
The Whitehaven and Furness Junction Railway opened its first section of line from Whitehaven to Bootle on July 1st, 1850.

July 29.
F. and R. W. Littleboy, Newport Pagnell.
July 30 to August 1.
Samuel Ward Jnr, London.
N. V. S. Pochin, Leicester and Caius Coll, Cambridge.
Came from Lodore to Buttermere, then over Scale Force, Red Pike, High Crag on to Scarf Gap over Black Sail to here - now off over Rossett Ghyll and Dungeon Ghyll and on to Lodore.
Watendlath Beck flows into Blea Tarn, descends through a ravine, past Watendlath village, down a rocky gorge between the Gowder and Shepherd's Crags and creates, after heavy rain, the Lodore Falls.

August 7.
There were stones and groans
And laughing and chaffing,
As we came over Black Sail
To the Wastwater Vale,
Getting wet in the Gills
And dry on the hills,
Having dined and drunk well,
Now we're off oer Scafell.
Ernest Price, London.
W. E. Rae, London.
H. Wrightson, London.
Wastwater is about one mile and a half from Nether Wasdale, where Will Ritson, one of the county's most colourful characters, is buried.

August 7.
J. H. Westcott, Philadelphia, U.S.A.

Henry S. Green, Manchester.

Of Mrs Tyson's kindness, and attention,
So many folks already have made mention,
That on their merits to make further comment,
The thought ne'er strikes me for a single moment,

But the one wish at least, escapes me never,
That both these virtues may go on for ever.
B.D.B.

The above is nothing but rot;
If you want to feel rather hot,
Get your clothes wet through and then borrow,
Mr Tyson's coat till tomorrow.
If you don't then feel very jolly,
Tell me I'm a fool for my folly.
W.R.

B. D. Beever, Manchester.

W. Rycroft, Bowdon, Cheshire.
W. Tidy, London.
W. T. Nevill, 1742 The Strand, London.

Passed over Sty Head, arrived here and was most kindly and
hospitably entertained by Mr and Mrs Tyson.

Oh how we did hail
The house Wastdale
Where good Dame Tyson doth dwell!
How goodie was she
To G. W., and me
And therefore her kindness I'll tell!
George William Holmes, Sowerby Bridge, Yorkshire.
John Holmes.
*There are two rain gauges at Sty Head, which are read on the first
day of each month and the figures sent to the meteorological
office.*

August 8.
John Clements, Liverpool.
August 9.
William Knight, United College, St Andrews, NB.
W. O. Steinthal, Owens College, Manchester.
E. M. Stochr, Alderley Edge, Cheshire.
O. H. Stochr, Rugby School, Warwickshire.
J. Henry Ball, London.

Came from Buttermere over Scarf Gap and Black Sail Passes,
reached Mrs Tysons at 3 p.m. Started at 4.30, climbed Great Gable
direct, scaling both peaks in succession by Rock Lichen (N.B. don't
attempt it without having a sure foot and steady head). Saw
Windermere, Langdale Pikes, Scafell Pikes, Helvellyn, Blencathra,
Skiddaw, Crummock Water, Grasmoor, Solway Firth, Scottish
Coast, Isle of Man, Jerusalem and Madagascar and North and South

America.
Richard F. Jupp, Blackheath.
E. B. and M. Jupp, Blackheath.

Mr and Mrs Heavisides, Stockton on Tees.
Walked from Buttermere via Scarff Gap and Black Sail Passes, time
occupied, 5 hours. Had a capital tea at Mrs Tyson's and should have
liked to have stayed, but are pushing on for Windermere.
August 11.
Arrived here from Keswick, after walking through the Sty Head Pass
in error, ten hours without a bite, returned next morning via Black
Sail Pass and Scarf Gap.
G. B. Dunsford, Liverpool.
Jon. C. Stead Jnr.

J. D. Sclater Booth, Balliol, Oxford.
C. L. Sclater Booth, Winchester.
From Buttermere, return there August 12th.

J. A. and H. Brown, Leeds.
The Hon. Tom Dudley, Dudley Hall.

August 15.
H. G. Ohlsen, Newcastle upon Tyne.
Thomas M. Conradi, Newcastle upon Tyne.
August 14 to 15.
Theodore Drew, London.
E. A. Cousins, Exeter College, Oxford.
August 16.
T. H. Grose, all from Queens College, Oxford.
E. M. Walker.
J. F. Longrigg.
R. Pontey.
August 20.
F. W. Bragger, Birkenhead.
H. Fox, Birkenhead.
From Keswick to Buttermere, over Scarf Gap and Black Sail Passes,
arrived here at 8 p.m. and were hospitably entertained by Mrs
Tyson. Weather fine.
*The road from Borrowdale to Buttermere is over Honister Pass. This
was the route of the four-in-hands. The horses had to be in tip-top
condition to pull the coaches up the steep ascent. The coachmen
would ask the younger passengers to leave the coach and walk up the
steepest part.*

August 11 to 20.
Rev. W. L. and Mrs Newham, Barrow on Soar, Leics.
Miss G. D. Newham.
Mr Darrall Newham.

Mr and Mrs Wike, Leicester.
William Howes, Barrow on Soar, Leics.

Rhodes Townend, Bradford.
Jon. R. Crabtree,   do
Samuel B. Dixon,   do
August 21.
J. Walter Stead, Athletic Club, Leeds.
Thomas Greaves, Oulton, Leeds.
August 23.
John McArthur Macmillan, Whitehaven.
James Christian, Yeorton Hall, Beckermet.
The church of St John, in the lovely village of Beckermet, was built in 1810, and the register dates from 1733.

August 24.
I. T. Greenwood, Coventry.
F. G. Greenwood,   do
W. G. Greenwood, Coventry.
August 25 to 26.
Corbet S. Catty, London.
M. D. Sayers, Tunbridge Wells.
Charles N. S. Catty, London.
Very much pleased with Dame Tyson's excellent accommodation and attention. From and back to Grasmere, via Angle Tarn and Langdale.
August 27.
J. Hudson Scott, Wigton, Cumb.
S. Swalwell, Dipton, Newcastle upon Tyne.
T. F. Hemsley, Hartlepool.

Today we have journeyed from Keswick,
The morning it dawned rather wet.
We purposed to mount upon Skiddaw,
But the mist changed the plans we had set.
We sauntered about all the morning,
Expecting the mist would ascend,
But Skiddaw still kept her grey cap on;
Our steps to the Lake we did wend.

We hired a boat for four shillings,
And paddled our way to Lodore.
The falls were delightful to look on,
The like we hadn't witnessed before.
The rain had been so continuous.
The water so plenteous and free
Rolled down with such roaring and tumult
'Mong boulders and rocks and green tree.

We next turned our steps up to Rosthwaite,
And found an hospitable Inn;
We regaled ourselves and were rested;
Though they sell not brandy or gin.
We then set our faces upvaleward
And crossed the steep path at Sty Head;
The path was both rocky and awkward;
The sky was as sodden as lead.

We found a good home with Mrs Tyson,
Who lives in the village below.
Now all who are languid and weary,
Just call at this house as you go.
You'll find with her every comfort,
You'll find a good table as well
I'd warmly advise you to try it.
It's a neat and homely hotel.
J. Hudson Scott, August 26th, 1879.

August 28.
Chr. Horner, Hull.
Richard Steenberg, Newcastle upon Tyne.

I. V. Salvage, Guys Hospital, London.
A. I. Dalton,   do
Were provided with a change of clothes, having arrived wet through
and were treated kindly by Mr and Mrs Tyson.

August 29.
O who can tell how hard it is to climb
The steep where Fame's proud temple shines afar.
Thus sang the poet Beattie in his time,
And passing years have failed its truth to mar.
But still to mount old Scafell's lofty pike
Mid rain and mist and hurricane of wind,
Is not forsooth a task which all will like,
At least small pleasure in the trip I find.
Today we scarce had passed Great Ends huge mass,
When drifting mist enveloped all the scene,
And fearful gales blew oer the tufted grass,
Driving the Tarn, which calm erewhile had been.
Yet on we went, 'Excelsior' our cry,
From cairn to cairn we toiled—from crag to crag;

While denser grew the mist, till by and by,
We needed the sure foot of goat or stag.
For sudden gusts of wind oftimes misplaced
The normal centre of our gravity,
Upset our equilibrium and graced

65

Some boggy fell with head, where feet should be.
We reached the narrow edge athwart the Pike,
But farther could not go, for all the gales
Of heaven seemed met to blast and downward strike
Us from the heights into the unseen vales.
Prostrate we clung for very life to earth;
Had we but loosed our grasp upon the cliff
Our utmost strength to stand were no more worth
Than one man's power, the Bowder Stone to lift.
But soon there came a lull — one moment brief —
And back we sprang upon the wider ground,
Hastening our steps to each cairn we perceive.

Now clinging once again, now onward bound.
At length we missed a pile of stones and know
That if no cairn is found to guide our way,
Efforts were vain to try to go below,
Until the coming darkness changed to day.
O heaven! the anguish of that dread suspense!
How anxiously we ran across the fell,
Piercing with eager gaze the mist so dense
I leave to abler pens than mine to tell.
But who can know the joy we travellers three
Felt when Old Sty Head's Tarn once more we passed,
Oasis in the desert could not be
More welcome — for our fears no longer last.
For soon we bent our steps to this fair spot
And neath this hospitable roof we find
Each comfort that the heart can wish,
And not a hostess in the district is more kind.
Henry E. Dudeney, London.

Joseph George Baker, Rotherham.
John Ackroyd, Mexboro, Rotherham.
J. W. and A. B. Sanderson, London.

September 2.
Mr and Mrs John D. Paul and party, Leicester.
Walter G. Bell, Cambridge.
Herbert C. Bell, London.
September 5.
Mr and Mrs William Evans, Leicester.
Rev. J. and Mrs Wood, Leicester.
Mrs R------- Leicester.
Miss Parsons, London.
Spent a week here and enjoyed it very much.
September 6.
Mr and Mrs F. Brandt and Miss K. H. Dobson, Ambleside.

September 8.
J. B. Mimmack, Secretary, Atalanta Harriers, London.
F. J. Blight, Captain, Atlanta Harriers, London.
Walter B. Slater, Secretary of C.R.M.I.S., London.
Thomas N. Ward, Ipswich. P.R.C.
Il coute beaucoup rester ici, garde to pouches Hic manere carumest, cave reticulum.
September 9.
Mr, Mrs, Miss and the Misses Lily, Nelly and Edie Forshaw, Brook House, Fulwood, Preston.
Made very comfortable.

H. P. Bridson, Belle Isle, Windermere, (of Mag's Coll, Oxford).
C. P. MacCarthy, Trinity College, Cambridge.
September 11.
Percy Stanley, London, W.
H. Cockerell, North Weald, Epping, Sussex.

Joseph B. Ellis, Newcastle upon Tyne.
William B. Ellis,   do
Joseph Ellis, Jnr.   do
John Mould,   do
James Hindhough,   do
Came here from Dungeon Ghyll in a most dreadful downpour of rain. There was thick mist all the way. We lost our way near to Sty Head Pass and could not find the track so came down the face of the mountain being guided by the stream. The boys did well and never complained.
After the death of that famous Lakeland personality, Will Ritson, a small waterfall above the Wastwater Hotel was named the 'Ritson Force' in his memory in 1890.

September 13.
W. N. Shaw, Cambridge.
Mary Shaw, Birmingham.
F. H. Shaw,   do
E. James Shaw, do
C. A. Vince, Repton.
James Hasder, Birmingham.
John Bright, Birmingham.
September 15.
Mrs, Mr and Miss Abraham, Grassendale Park, Liverpool.
September 17.
John B. Laycock, Keighley.
John W. Laycock,   do

Dr. M. P. Read, spent three very enjoyable days here and can highly recommend Mrs Tyson's fare.

67

Miss Eliza Williamson, Stockton on Tees.
Visited here on Sept. 16th/19th.
September 19.
Mr and Miss Davison, Manchester.
September 23.
Robert Pattinson, Carlisle.
W. Taylor Herd, Dublin.
Charles Holroyd, Leeds.
W. Charles Copperthwaite, York.
Very much pleased with our kind reception.
September 24.
Mr. H. Carpenter Jnr. Third Visit.
Mrs Carpenter.

Edward H. Vize, Rock Ferry, Cheshire.
Found Miss Williamson a very pleasant young lady (as on Sept. 17th).
September 25.
George E. Hall, Rock Ferry, Cheshire.
Everything here neat, comfortable and pleasant. Dame Tyson the same. Hope to be here again.

I concur in the same. E. H. Vize.
September 26.
M. E. Hughes-Hughes, Highbury, London.
Whose experience differs toto coelo from that of the party who wrote in this book on the 8th inst.

John Clark, Sheffield.
William Bennett, Sheffield.
Arrived here last evening and met with a motherly welcome from kind Mrs Tyson, whose attentions were fully appreciated. Left in pouring rain (and mist on the tops) intending to reach Grasmere tonight via Sty Head Pass and Rossett Ghyll. Two jolly friends as of old, when we were boys together.

Miss Eliza Williamson, Stockton on Tees.
Paid her aunt and uncle a visit for the first time in her life and stayed a fortnight. During her stay climbed Great Gable and came back by Sty Head Pass and enjoyed it very much and did more than my uncle Mr Tyson ever expected. Hoping to surprise him more my next visit, and I hope I won't be so long in coming again.

Leon Atkins is a flat
You may all depend on that
For to look at his productions
Is enough to make one shout ructions
The charge is moderate
The fare is good

I'd stop longer
If I could.
Ode to Mrs Tyson of Wasdale.

From Keswick through several bogs and brooks. Got soaked through
in the valleys and hung out to dry on the mountain tops. Where the
water either evaporated or turned to ice to thaw again, when I
arrived in the valley. Result—No more of Wasdale for me.
T. C. Summers, Mile End Road, London.

Leon Atkins, of Mile End Road, London, and Tommy Summers of
somewhere abouts, started from Keswick for Ambleside, via Scafell
Pike; lost our way, one fine day in September '79. When we found
our whereabouts we were opposite Mrs Tyson's. She coaxed us into
her isolated, antiquated, hereditary mansion, which, she states, has
been in their illustrious family seven centuries. When we first made
the acquaintance of our destined hostess, we were rather shy of her
lupine looks, but we finally took to her as did Romulous and Remus.

'Idle Men and Boys are found,
Standing on the devils ground.'
So do I mean it.
Satan finds some mischief still for idle hands to do.

There is a house in Wasdale Vale,
Where Mrs Tyson tells a tale,
About her antecedents,
They were a very long lived race,
Who used to drag out in this place,
A doctorless existence.

Now to begin to tell our tale,
For subjects we begin to quail,
But we must do our duty.
So to begin we shall relate,
Some items of our awful fate,
And wind up with its praises.

Now first of all, from Keswick started,
A very small, a little party.
Minus guides, two young starters.
Through bog, through brook, nothing daunted.
These young sprites, wet footed flaunted,
Onward to some destination.

Our object truly was Scafell Pike,
And to Ambleside before the night,
But this was not our fortune.
When past the Pike we bungling sped,

I would tell you more, but I'm going to bed.
So Goodnight.
You don't know what you can do till you try.
Tommy Summers and Leon Atkins.

James Robinson, Westover Street, London.
Benjamin Smenstsey of the above place.
Mr and Mrs J. A. Forster, London.
C. A. Falcon, Nuthurst.
C. W. Archibald, Blackheath.

September 3 to October 6.
Frederick, William and Emily Iacomb, Huddersfield.
September 30 to October 7.
F. H. Bowring, Lincolns Inn, London.
October 7.
Herbert Hodges, Dorchester, Dorset.
October 24.
Mr and Mrs John H. Downes, Glasgow.

Charles I. Richardson, Gateshead on Tyne.
R. M. Richardson.
Left Dungeon Ghyll, knapsack on back, having first got a good specimen of Hymruophyllum Wilsonii from the Ghyll, and made our way up Rossett Gill. When halfway up were greeted by a downpour of rain, snow and mist and when we reached the Great End the ground was white—an inch thick. Here the sun came out and ie clouds disappeared, so had a magnificent view. Descended by Lingmell on to the Honister road and nearly missed this comfortable retreat. Luck was, with us however, and we were made recipients of Mrs Tyson's much, and deservedly praised, hospitality. Would have enjoyed a longer visit, but must go on to Keswick (via Black Sail, Scarf Gap, Buttermere and Crummock), where we stay for a few days.
November 5.
Mr and Mrs George Mannering, South Norwood.
December 27.
The undersigned left Aikton for Whitehaven thence to Wasdale Head, and are so sorry their stay is so short, trusting soon to pay them another visit for a longer time. Mr and Mrs Tyson have been so kind and affectionate towards us.
Isaac Susannah Williamson.

1880

March 7.
Alfred Back.
H. R. King.
March 26.
Arthur Monro.
A. B.
H. R. K.

T. Christie, Rossall, Fleetwood.
H. White, Lincold College, Oxford.
March 27.
W. C. Sunley.
G. F. Vernon.
E. Hulton.

H. M. Ormesby, Rossall.
C. B. Ogden, Rossall.

William Colfox, Bridport.
T. A. Colfox,   do

Fritz Delius, Bradford.
Arrived here after a killing pull over Black Sail Pass, but a good tea restored us. Start tomorrow for Langdale over Sty Head Pass, we expect to have a tough pull, and expect to get to Windermere in a day or two very thin.

Pillar Rock is a climb for experts and the experienced rock-climbers, while Pillar is a safe and comparatively easy climb, taking only some 90 minutes from Black Sail Pass. The Pillar Rock was climbed in 1875 by the Rev. 'Steeple' Jackson when aged 79 years. The nickname was because in 1861 he had climbed to the top of his own church spire to repair a weather-cock, not because of his rock climbing ability. Rev. Jackson wrote the following jingle to commemorate his feat:

Who has not heard of Steeple Jack
That lion-hearted Saxon?
Though I'm not he, he was my sire
For I am Steeple Jackson.
He attempted to climb Pillar Rock again three years later but never
returned. His body was recovered two days later. He had died not
from a fall but from a heart attack.

March 28.
F. Elliott, Bradford.
H. Speight, Bradford.
William Carter Best, Darlington.
T. Liddell, Huddersfield.
T. H. Partridge, Huddersfield.
March 29 to 30.
William Braddon, Cheatham Hill, Manchester.
Edward Challender,   do
C. B. Andrew,   do
James Wilson,   do
March 30.
W. Thorburn, Medical School, Owens College, Victoria Univ.
Stopped here on the 31st, being prevented from ascending Scafell
by heavy rain. N.B...a billiard table would be a great advantage.

March 30 to April 1.
C. Archibald Scott, St Johns College, Cambridge.
W. E. Sawers Scott, Owens College, Manchester.
April 2.
Horace Walker.
W. C. Slingsby.
C. M. Fletcher.
G. F. Vernon.
F. Hardcastle.
I. Walker Hartley.
E. Hulton.
April 13.
F. E. Wilson, Southport.
C. Wilson, Edinburgh.
April 15.
H. E. Lees, Fettes College, Edinburgh.
From Windermere by Scafell Pike.
April 18.
J. Mason, and H. R. King.
May.
Mrs. A. Lightfoot, Hensingham.
Mrs. Lightfoot, Crankland.
Miss Sharp, Briar House.
Hensingham is in the Whitehaven district and stands on the
Egremont road. The church of St. John built in 1791 was demolished

in 1913. The new church was built the same year upon a site given by the Earl of Lonsdale.

May 11.
Mr and Mrs George, and their four daughters
Came for a visit to these Wasdale waters —
Had they stayed contentedly at Eskdale Green,
Good Mrs Tyson they would never have seen —
But here from Eskdale they came for a change.
To see of the mountains a different range.

One day Black Sail these girls surmounted -
One by one on a pony, when tired they mounted
But when at Nelson's arrived tired they,
What! Return again that dreadful way!
Dear Mrs Tyson, say can't you find
A road leading homeward more to our mind?
So the kindly Maw, these dear girls to please
Brought them round by Sty Head, their tired feet to ease!

May 12.
William I'Anson, Darlington.
Edward W. I'Anson, London.
May 17.
F. W. Baynes, Blackburn.
D. Charles Baynes, Blackburn.
May 18.
Henry J. Pearson, Notts.
Charles E. Pearson, Notts.
John Orton, MD., Notts.
Arthur L. Rogers, Nottingham.
May 19.
G. H. Pentland, all of Dublin.
C. Barrington.
W. N. Barrington.
G. Wright.

Walter H. Lee, Manchester.
May 20.
S. Sowater, Nottingham.
Joseph Higgins, Manchester.
J. Morton, Whitby.
J. Addison, Bradford.
Joseph Peacock, Armley, Leeds.
Robert Locke, Beeston Hill, Leeds.
James Mills, New Wortley, Leeds.
Mr. and Mrs. Embleton, Hurworth on Tees.

J. M. Perry, Nottingham.

H. R. Thorpe,   do
Stayed several days at Mrs Tyson's and were much pleased with their visit.
May 22.
Mrs. Carter, Knottingley, Yorks.
Mrs. Percival,   do
Miss Senior,   do
Miss Langhorne, Howden, Yorks.
May 24 to 25.
I. E. Weeks, Bromley, Kent.
F. Weeks.
June 10.
L. J. Donaldson, London.
H. L. Drew, London.
June 15.
Misses Morris and Harrison, Runcorn, Cheshire.
June 15.
A. Noel Newling, Liverpool.
J. H. Couzens, London.
From Buttermere via Scarf Gap and Buttermere Passes.
In many places in the Lake District, including Buttermere, when anyone died, two persons from every house within a certain well defined boundary were invited to the funeral. The houses within that circle were termed The Laitin.

June 18.
Mr and Mrs John Martin arrived here yesterday from Dungeon Ghyll Hotel over Rossett Gill, Scafell Pikes and Lingmell and leave today for Keswick via Black Sail and Scarf Gap and Honister Passes. Have been exceedingly comfortable at Mrs Tyson's.

William Illingworth Allison, Leeds.
Above Dungeon Ghyll, on the Langdale side, are Stickle Tarn and Pavey Ark, which has several good rock climbs.

June 21.
Mr and Mrs H. Y. Stanger, Nottingham.
June 22.
Mrs. Calvert, St Bees.
E. S. Benson, Preston.
Mrs. Colebank, Black Beck Cottage.
John Russell, Holmrook.
Were well refreshed by kind Dame Tyson.
June 19 to 23.
A. Appleton, Trinity College, Cambridge.
F. M. Appleton, Warrington.
Could not have been more kindly and hospitably treated by Mr. and Mrs. Tyson.

June 22 to 23.
Mr. and Mrs. B. W. Wood of Hull — having walked over Sty Head Pass, stayed a night here, before resuming their walk to Buttermere and found it a most comfortable place.

June 26.
Fred Althorp, Bradford.
Walked from Buttermere via Scarf Gap and Black Sail Pass and found Mrs Tyson's to be literally a land flowing with milk (cream) and honey.
Arthur Binns, Bradford.

June 29.
James T. Fulcher, Warrington.
John Glover, Warrington.
D. Holdsworth, Gosforth.
Gosforth, a small town, is situated five miles west of Wastwater. The hall was originally built in the reign of Charles II by Robert and Isabel Copley.

June 30.
The undersigned arrived here from Keswick via Sty Head Pass, wet through, but as Mrs Tyson was able to supply us with dry clothes and a capital dinner, our troubles were soon at an end.
Campbell Cooke, London.
R. C. Cooke.

July 1.
F. G. Marlow, Frizington.
Thomas G. Marlow.
Missed Black Sail — came between Kirkfell and Gable. Followed the Beck. Had a narrow escape from falling down Hill Ghyll.
When crossing Sty Head or Black Sail, it is advisable to have company, as there is always the real danger of being caught in a cloud.

July 4.
James Wilding, Preston.
James Kendal, Preston.
W. H. Sharples, Preston.
During our stay here we were well attended and moderately charged.

July 5.
William Hillier, (M. Invt. Inst), Battersea Park, London.

July 6.
Thos. Collinson, Halifax.
Jonathan Ba----   do

July 7.
We arrived here this evening from Keswick via Buttermere, Scarp Gap and Black Sail, and after a row to the end of Wastwater, returned refreshed. Intend climbing Scafell Pikes in morning and proceeding to Coniston.
Arthur W. Wade, Leeds.

Mrs. Wade.

Hainsworth Wade, Leeds.

July 8.

T. I. Wright, Gateshead.

Mr. and Mrs. S. Woodman, Ramsgate.

July 10.

Lieut Colonel I. R. Campbell.

William A. Kennedy-Jostling.

July 15.

Walter J. Davidson, Gateshead.

Michael N. Davidson.

July 17.

George R. Ward, Newcastle upon Tyne.

July 19.

Urban P. Giles, London, arrived from Keswick and found everything very comfortable here, in fact felt very much at home.

July 20.

Mr. and Mrs. E. Godfree, Chiswick, London.

July 19 to 21.

Edward L. Barnard, London.

July 22.

Samuel Kay, Sheffield.

July 21 to 22.

A. P. Harrison, Newcastle upon Tyne.

Misses Harrison,   do

July 19 to 23.

Charles H. May, Pilgrim House, South Weald, Essex.

July 23.

Rev. Tilden Smith and Mrs. Tilden Smith, London.

Arthur F. Lake, London.

Herbert N. Carr, London.

July 27.

Francis H. Irvine, London.

P. A. Holland, London.

From Windermere to Keswick by Buttermere.

Keswick has long been dominated by Skiddaw, the summit of which has often been used for lighting beacons. The Southeys and their friends, the Wordsworths, made a bonfire on Skiddaw to celebrate the victory at Waterloo in 1815.

July 26.

C. Lowry, Christ Church College, Oxford.

C. Cannan,   do

A. L. Mumm, Christ Church College.

J. E. King, Lincoln College, Oxford.

G. Hastings, Silsden.

C. Hastings,   do

Mr. and Mrs. F. Strickland, Hastings.

July 28.
Fred Shorrock, Blackburn.
Tom Shorrock, Blackburn.
Frank Shorrock, Blackburn.
John Swift, Sheffield.
Arthur Dean, Sheffield.
July 29.
William Sessions, York.
E. Vipont Brown, York.
July 30.
G. A. Carter, London.
Bernard R. Sullivan, London.
A. J. Hall, Aston, Near Birmingham.
August 1.
W. H. Liddle, London.
R. Broom, London.
F. Lang, London.
Tom Bennett, London.
August 2.
Abel Higginbottom, Sheffield.
R. Lister, Liverpool.
J. E. Lister.
J. N. Lister.
Joseph L. Threlkeld, Grange in Borrowdale.
At Grange in Borrowdale, a coarse apron is known as a 'brat'. There is a saying that, when it rains on Maudlin [Magdalen] Day, August 2nd, 'Jenny Maudlin is bleaching her brat.'

August 2 to 3.
Thomas P. Hodgson, Liverpool.
Samuel Anderson, Whitehaven.
Thomas Nicholas Griffin, Whitehaven.
Apart from Newcastle and York, Whitehaven, as late as 1816, was recognised as the largest town in the North of England.

August 3.
S. R. Carr, London.
W. H. Harding, London.
From Mrs. Tyson's at Gillthwaite over Black Sail to Mrs Tyson's at Wasdale Head. Thence to Ulpha (What do you think).
(This entry is complemented by a sketch — see page 105).

Four and a half miles north of Broughton-in-Furness, Ulpha is on the Duddon, where an ancient stone bridge crosses the river. The parish is beautifully situated among mountains some of which, are covered to their summits with trees.

August 3 to 4.
H. W. Stock, Rectory, Windermere.

C. H. Stock.

L. Stock.

A. H. Stable, Rectory, Windermere. *When the railway from Kendal to Windermere was opened in 1847, it was planned to run the line along the lake shore to Low Wood, but Wordsworth violently opposed this proposal. The terminus was built at Birthwaite, below Orrest Head.*

August 4.
J. Henry Ball, London.
William A. Ball, London.
August 5.
Samuel Wakefield, Liverpool.
Walter Humphreys, Stockport.
August 6.
John D. Sims, Ipswich.
Edward Ranson, Norwich.

J. Cartland Barrett-Walter, London.

W. S. Hume, Ferndale, Tunbridge Wells.
Miss Hume,   do
August 7 to 9.
William Parr, Ellerbrook, Near Ormskirk.
Annie Parr, same address.
August 8 to 9.
W. B. Ferguson, Christ Church, Oxford.
August 9.
John Armstrong, Oldham.
Frank Hepworth, Oldham.
Charles Hague, Oldham.
John Hepworth, Oldham.
August 9 to 10.
Mr. and Mrs. O. H. Howarth, London.
Harold MacFarlane, Southport.
James Ridpath, South Hampstead, London.
August 3 to 10.
Mr. and Mrs. Frederick Howell, Birmingham. A most pleasant time and comfortable home. Scawfell on the 7th, descent straight over Lingmell. *On the summit of Scafell Pike, set into a cairn, is a memorial bearing the names of the men of the Lake District who fell in the two World Wars. One of the highest war memorials in the world, it was presented by Lord Leconfield to the National Trust.*

August 10.
The following coves walked from Keswick to Buttermere via Honister Pass. Visited Scale Force, bumped over Scarf Gap (MET A BISHOP!!!!) and splashed over Black Sail. (Hint for enterprising

inn-keeper — steamer between Scarf Gap and Wasdale in wet weather).

For the goodness of her Hyson
We must praise Mrs. Tyson.

— Charles Stephenson, Bd.

Harold Hebblethwaite, BNS, YN Union, BGSCC, DS.
James Robert Thackrah, Halifax.
William H. Hatch, Halifax.
(*The drawing which embellishes the Visitors' Book at this point is reproduced on page 106*).

August 11.
The following entry is written in Greek, and then translated:-
Where (can we find such), hosts (as these?)
          At Mrs. Tyson's
— H. H.
   C. S.
   J. R. T.
   W. H. H.

August 12.
F. I. Greenwood, Coventry.
R. Rigg, Coventry.
August 13.
Gertrude Stead, Waterloo, Liverpool.
A. H. Stead,   do
E. A. Stead,   do

John Glaisyer, York.
Eleanor Glaisyer, Brighton.
Harold Glaisyer, Brighton.
Henry Glaisyer, Birmingham.

W. M. Dingwall, Charterhouse.
F. A. Dingwall, Merchant Taylors.

E. E. Edwards, Liverpool.
Frank Edwards, Liverpool.

John H. Pemblebury, ------------

H. H. Pumphrey, Bromyard.
August 17.
Mr. and Mrs. Edward Wingfield, London.

August 18.

Francis James Dingle, Heames House, Worcester.

John Dingle of the same address.

Arrived from Drigg last night and after various disappointments, at Strands and Wasdale Head Inn, were very glad to find a resting place here.

August 11 to 18.

Miss C. Townsend, St Michael's Vicarage, London.

Miss M. Townsend.

Stephen Townsend.

August 19.

Walter Brownridge, Leeds.

E. Winpenny, Holbeck, Nr Leeds.

Basil Mott, London.

Syd. A. Grinson, Leicester.

Alexander MacIndoe, Glasgow.

William L. MacIndoe, Glasgow.

Edgar John Swayne, Salisbury.

A. C. Beckton, Didsbury, Manchester.

E. Beckton, Didsbury, Manchester.

G. Pilkington, Manchester.

August 21.

Saturday, August 21st, Joseph Knott and R. A. Punshon, of Sunderland left Buttermere 9 a.m., and arrived here via Scarf Gap and Black Sail Pass at 1.15. Thoroughly paid out. Weather hot, awful. Left here about 4.p.m., for Keswick via Sty Head and Seatoller.

Ethel Brown, Clifton College, Bristol.

Mary Stowell-Talbot, Castletown, Isle of Man.

Edith Brown, Clifton College, Bristol.

Rev. T. E. and Mrs. Brown, Clifton College, Bristol.

August 22.

James Duncalf, Oxton, Cheshire.

John G. Scott, 154 Tufnell Park Road, London.

Thomas Hargreaves, Douglas, Isle of Man.

J. H. Corson, Halifax.

Spent a most delightful Sabbath, cheered by glorious weather, and the unbounded hospitality of Mrs. Tyson.

August 23.

S. A. Tyson, London.

Mrs. Tyson, London.

Mrs. Layton, Dalston.

Master J. Tyson, London.

After a most delightful walk, over the mountains, returned to Mrs Tyson's and had a most enjoyable tea.

Dalston is a large village on the banks of the river Caldew four and a half miles south west of Carlisle. The church of St Michael,

originally built in the 12th century, is of mixed style. The chancel is
Early English and a portion of some of the walls is Transition
Norman.

August 23.
Lizzie Kendall, Clifton.
H. M. Watson, Clifton.
T. Green, London.

Fell in here after a 36 mile walk by Coniston, from Ambleside and
were very much refreshed with a hearty tea.
Ben. J. Howarth.

Doth the above hand shake, with unusual exercise.
Arthur Palmer, Doncaster.

Anne Smith, Walham Green, Fulham.
Martha J. Proud, Maryport.
These two ladies were accompanied by two of the biggest and
smallest torments that ever crossed Sty Head Pass, nothing but the
excessive courage of the ladies prevented them being drowned in
Wastwater. Beware of boats on Wastwater, see that you are
furnished with broken oars and a tin to bale out the water. August
24th 1880.
Still the 24th. This is all written after a hearty breakfast in Mrs.
Tyson's best style. This accounts for the verbosity of the ladies.
M. Williamson, Maryport.

J. W., H. C., Annie Smith and Martha Brown,
Over Sty Head Pass came rolling down.
It was such fun to see the splatter,
When at the bottom, they looked like batter.
Jimmiwhiskies, they enjoyed the chat.
Especially when looking at Mrs. Tyson's cat.

J. W. Brookes, Eltham, Kent.
Stayed here on the night of the 23rd August and was extremely
comfortable.
S. Watkinson, York.
J. Watkinson, York.
August 25.
C. Lewes, London.
Tom Langdon.

Edward Hunt, Harmondworth, Middlesex.
William Bradley, Cowper Villa, Dover.
Edmund Bradley.
A. M. Bradley.

Robert A. Penny, Brighton.
Charles A. Penny, Darlington.
Total 2d. Settled A. Tyson.
Surely two 'A' Pennies make one Penny - Audited and found incorrect.
H. G.

August 26.
Maurice Day, Wichenford.
I. G. Johnson, Bedford.

John Elwell, Beverley, Yorkshire.
F. C. D. Burt, Beverley, Yorkshire.

Francois C. Du Bart, Rue de Rivoli, Paris and Gloucester.

Charles L. Bragger, Tranmere, Cheshire.

Tilden John Bisseker, of Birmingham, has spent two very pleasant days here.
August 27.
J. Bernard Junior, Huyton, Liverpool.
S. Veevers, Huyton, Liverpool.
G. W. Drew, Fulham, London.
F. R. Nuttall, St Helens, Lancs.
H. Galton, St Helens, Lancs.
En route from Keswick to Buttermere via Scafell Pike and Black Sail.
August 30.
I. T. Marsh, Rainhill, Lancs.
John Allen, London.
August 31.
T. F. Lardelli, 8 Surbiton Terrace, Surbiton.
M. E. Hughes-Hughes, 5 Highbury Quadrant, London.

T. A. Tugwell, Scarborough.
G. A. S. Frank.
W. H. Land.
September 1.
F. Austin, Culverlea, Winchester.

H. Milton Savage and W. H. Savage, Liverpool, arrived here from Buttermere, August 31st.
September 2.
Herbert Shaw, Lees, Manchester.
Harold Shaw, Lees, Manchester.
September 3.
Edgar Lucas, Streatham Lane, Upper Tooting.

Mrs. Edgar Lucas, Streatham Lane, Upper Tooting.
September 2.
J. Bradbury, Sheffield.
M. I. Hunter, Sheffield.
September 3.
Miss Clifford, Beechcroft House, Edgbaston.
C. W. Clifford, Inner Temple, London.
Very much pleased with the hospitable entertainment here.
September 2.
Wilson Dobson, Great Crosby, Liverpool.
Mrs. W. Dobson.
Found everything very nice and Mr. and Mrs. Tyson most kind and attentive. Stayed three days and was pleased with the scenery and the drive from Calder Bridge.

Before the church of St Cuthberts at Calder Bridge was built in 1890 services were held in the railway station waiting room and goods shed.
September 2.
H. Milton Savage and W. H. Savage started early in the morning for Scafell Pikes, but the weather turning out very wet and cold and the mountains being covered with mist were obliged to turn back drenched. Were made very comfortable by a change of clothes, which Mrs. Tyson provided.

Fritz Machenhauer, Muhlhausen im Odenwald (Germany).
The villages of Nether Wasdale and Wasdale Head, in the shadow of the Scafell Pikes, celebrated Stirrup Sunday on the 25th Sunday after Trinity. After eating rice pudding for their dinner, the villagers all repeated this rhyme:
Stir up we beseech thee the pudding in the pot,
Stir't up we beseech thee, and keep it all hot.

September 3.
E. Potter, Manchester.
T. N. Toller, Manchester.
John Derry, Bourne.
Jesse Stow, Morton, Lincs.
H. Stephenson, Newton Kyne and Leeds.
J. H. Inglebury, Tadcaster.
Fearnley Swift, Bradford.
Ben Lee, Yeadon, Leeds.
Thomas Norfolk, Bradford and Tockwith.
H. Bradley, Bradford.
September 4.
Alfred M. Appleton, Durham.
J. Mawson, Durham.

John Mould, Newcastle upon Tyne.

Joseph B. Ellis.
John William Ellis.
James Hindhaugh Junior.
We had a narrow escape from the hotel lower down and feel thankful to providence for guiding us here.
September 5.
Rev. J. Slade, Little Levin Parsonage, Bolton le Moor.
Constance E. Slade.
Arthur T. Slade.
Very comfortably accommodated.

Ernest O. Wooler, Batley, Yorkshire.
Charles C. Wooler.
Edmund Hemmingway.

William B. Webster, Darlington.
Joseph Brady, Darlington.
September 6.
Gerard M. Mason, Watford.
Rodney C. J. Swinhoe, Cheltenham.
August 23 to September 6.
F. H. Bowring, Lincolns Inn, London.
Frederick H. Bowring, 1823-1918, a native of the west country and Fellow of Trinity College, Oxford, resembled in appearance the poet Tennyson. Bowring often stayed with the Tysons at Row Farm, for he was a confirmed fell-walker and hill wanderer, which activities were the forerunners of mountaineering and rock climbing in the Lake District. It was he who introduced Walter Parry Haskett-Smith, later to be acknowledged as the 'Father of British Climbing', to John Wilson Robinson of Lorton, who became one of the county's greatest climbers. Haskett-Smith and Robinson made one of the finest climbing teams ever known in the Lake District.

September 6.
M. Stude, Bombay.

Ed. S. Wise, Sussex.

Ada Jean Evans, London, and Mrs. Rea, Eskdale and Hope Rea, Eskdale.
Those dames in full rig,
Set out in a gig,
To drive here from Eskdale Green;
When they get back,
To routine and rack,
They will not wish they never had been. —A. J. E.

G. H. Drew; Grace Drew; Julia C. Drew; left Grasmere this morning,

came by Easedale Tarn, Angle Tarns, Esk Hause, and Sty Head, one
of the best walks in England. Slept here and on 7th September left
for Buttermere. Well content with our entertainment.

T. Child, London.
Chas. L. Devitt, London.
September 7.
William Thorpe, Little Head, Bradford, Yorkshire.
J. E. Mann, Lilycroft, Bradford.
A. Baxendale, Salterhebble, Halifax.

T. Wilmer Collier and Mrs. Collier have spent three very happy
weeks at Wasdale Head and received every kindness and attention
from Mr. and Mrs Tyson, leaving with regret.
Hoylake.

T. Gravely, Darlington.
Richard W. Brogden, London.
E. R. Mosley, Hastings.
Miss Ledger, Liverpool.
Miss A. Ledger, Liverpool.
Both spent a very pleasant afternoon and received every kindness,
from Mr. and Mrs. Tyson.

Dinely F. Tonge and Mrs. Lincoln.
*Wordsworth and De Quincey, with a party of anglers, and
accompanied by 12 ponies carrying their camping gear, travelled
through Eskdale to Wasdale in the summer of 1809. Here they spent
a week fishing in the lake, which is rich in game fish.*

September 7.
Rev. H. J. Hind, Woodcote House, Reading.
Walter Southern. Manchester.
A. W. Kindler, Stockton on Tees.
Cuthbert S. Thompson, Birmingham and Keswick.
A. G. Pettitt, Keswick.
R. Lindal, Nether Wasdale.
September 8.
Arthur Harrington-Hill. R.M.A., H.M.S. Penelope, Harwich.
September 9.
B. Scarf, Edgbaston, Warwickshire.

Scarf. B., accompanied by his children three,
Named respectively Charlie, Fred and Lillie,
Called in here hungry during a walking tour,
And put a lot of grub out of sight in an hour.

Now beat that if you can!

We are going to walk, where few people do—
through their own gaps (Scarf Gap).

Henry J. Bates, Sheffield.
J. Stanley Marshall, Sheffield.
September 9 to 10.
Mr. and Mrs. Lensche, Manchester.
W. M. Watt, Settle.
J. W. Chippett.
H. S. Beresford Webb, Settle.
Philip Barecroft.
September 12.
R. T. Blomfield and H. R. King.
William E. Chambers.
September 13.
Thomas Spencer, Leicester.
Philip Wright.
S. Lennard, Leicester.
Thomas Mitchell, Derby.
Walked from Lodore Hotel by Honister Crag and descended here by
the Beck between Kirkfell and Great Gable—a caution—anyone
coming that way keep to the right as high as can, so as to drop
down the Sty Head Pass. Very pleased with the attention given us
here.
Kirk Fell lies between Wasdale and Ennerdale and is little explored,
even in the high season. So if you are looking for solitude?

Mrs. and Miss Sampson, Hendon, London.
Miss C. E. Growse, Hendon.
After a very happy week in this dear old house are truly sorry to say
goodbye to Mr. and Mrs. Tyson, who have been most kind and
attentive in every way.

I. E. Norman, Clare College, Cambridge, and Northampton.
W. H. Turner, Rugby School, and Northampton.
Arrived here from Buttermere over Scarf Gap and Black Sail Pass
on September 17th. Found Wastwater the grandest lake in the whole
district, and came to the conclusion that good Dame Tyson was well
worthy of her long line of ancestors.

S. Murton, Trinity College, Cambridge.
A. E. Hawley of Leicester, walked on September 18th from
Buttermere over the hills beyond Scale Force, into Ennerdale and
on to Wasdale through Black Sail Pass, and arrived at this hospitable
house late at night, drenched through, where he received every
attention from the kind Mrs. Tyson.
The Eskdale and Ennerdale Pack of hounds was formed in 1883,
with Tommy Dobson as master and huntsman. Tommy was a native

*of Staveley near Kendal and moved to Eskdale, when he was 23, to
follow his trade as a bobbin-turner. There he started hunting with
his own two hounds, Cruiser and Charmer. Later he added more
hounds to lay the foundation of a proper pack. This was augmented
by the addition of individually owned local hounds. In return for a
small annual subscription from the local farmers and dalesmen,
Tommy and his pack hunted the predatory foxes.*

September 20.
I. Blakey, Leeds.
John Stead, Leeds.
Thomas S. Townend, London.
Mrs. T. Townend, London.
September 19 to 21.
A. G. Cumberland, Leicester.
September 22.
R. Chaddock Junior, Liverpool.
E. Kellick, Liverpool.
September 24.
Mr. Mulcaster, Northumberland.
Mr. Walter Mulcaster, Northumberland.
Stayed here from 19th to 24th, most comfortable and very glad to
find ourselves once more under Mrs. Tyson's hospitable roof.
September 25.
William Mitchell, London.
F. E. Wilson, London.
September 28.
J. W. Dowden, Merchiston, Castle School, Edinburgh.
Rev. Dr. Dowden, St Mary's Cathedral, Edinburgh.
Were made very comfortable by Mrs. Tyson, after a long walk from
Grasmere via Langdale and Rossett Gill.
*Grasmere village is an ideal centre to spend a holiday. It is
surrounded by easy walks to places of interest. Dove cottage and
Rydal Mount are two of Wordsworth's homes within easy walking
distance.*

September 30.
Rev. J. M. Easterling, Barnsley, Yorks.
E. Burchell Rodway, Ironbridge.
September 31.
Miss Holt, Liverpool.
Miss M. A. Smith, Tunbridge Wells.
(presumably this entry is in error for October 1).
October 3.
The Misses Simpson, Scawfell Hotel, Rosthwaite.
Mr. I. Briggs, Dovenby.
Mr. T. Wetherstone, Dovenby.
Mr. J. Simpson, Rosthwaite.
The treatment received is beyond description and they are lucky

indeed, that find their way to this hospitable domicile. — T. Weatherstone.

The village of Dovenby is 2½ miles from Cockermouth. Fifty years ago the master of the village school was paid £4 annually to give religious instruction to the children. Dovenby Hall, a mansion standing in a park of 52 acres, was formerly the seat of the Ballantyne-Dykes.

October 4 to 6.

J. Hoskins, Liverpool.
E. Hoskins, Liverpool.

October 6 to 8.

A. Rhodes, Greenwich, Kent.
No-one could wish to be more comfortable than with Mrs. Tyson and the pleasant time I passed at Wasdale Head will never be forgotten.

October 9.

James Shanks, Egremont.

1881

February 13.
Wilfred Ainslie, Windermere, both of us snowed in.
H. R. King.
March 23 to April 1.
H. R. King, Windermere.
March 23 to April 13.
H. R. King. BA., Exeter College, Oxford.
March 23 to April 7.
C. Lowry, Christ College, Oxford.
March 23 to April 30.
C. Cannan, Christ College, Oxford.
R. L. Knight, Christ Church College, Oxford.
Charles Cannan, Dean of Trinity College, Oxford, organised visits of students' parties during Easter vacations. The holiday spent at the Tysons combined climbing with reading sessions and discussion. After an evening meal in the farmhouse kitchen, the undergraduates, together with other guests, occupied the parlour. Here the discussion group got under way. Often present were Arnold Mumm, chief historian and registrar of the Alpine Club, and J. E. King, Corpus Christi College, later to become headmaster of Clifton School. They were regular visitors to the farmstead and enthusiastic climbers. Thomas De Quincey, a friend of Wordsworth, Coleridge and Southey, the Lake Poets, enjoyed these evenings in the parlour, almost as much as his zest for fell-walking.

April 2.
Eustace Hulton.
C. Picklington.
L. Picklington.
Horace Walker.
C. Lowry.
April 9.
C. P. Newcombe, Windermere.
Wilfred Ainslie, Windermere.
March 30 to April 13.
A. L. Mumm, Christ Church College, Oxford.

April 9 to 23.
E. N. P. Moor, MA., Balliol College, Oxford.
April 8 to 13.
W. King, Windermere.
April 15.
I. Walter.
H. Thorp.
H. C. Kendall, all from Windermere.
March 30 to April 15.
A. L. Mumm, Christ Church College, Oxford.
April 16.
W. J. Ellam, Manchester.
D. Johnson, Nottingham.
G. H. Seed, Manchester.
C. Wagner, Manchester.
April 17.
Sydney Mitchell, Solihull.
Phillip H. Willmot, Mosely, Birmingham.
George D. Willmot,   do
Arthur J. Mitchell, Solihull.
H. H. Mitchell, Rossall.
F. A. Willmot, Rossall.
April 18.
W. M. Shaw, Emmanuel College, Cambridge.
A. N. Marshall, Manchester.
Alfred Hopkinson, Manchester.
Edward Hopkinson, Manchester.
Albert Hopkinson, Manchester.
Charles Hopkinson, Manchester.

Mr. and Mrs. H. F. Salt, Eton College.
April 22.
Caleb Scott, Manchester.
Walter Scott, Manchester.

J. M. Tyson, London.
T. B. Tyson, London.
Arthur Huddart, Santon Bridge.
Hannah Mary Watson, Santon Bridge.
May 3.
A. Wilson Davies, Southport.
F. Wilson, Southport.
May 24.
H. W. Watson, Ghyll Bank, Whitehaven.
May 24 to 30.
F. H. Bowring, Lincolns Inn, London.
May 30.
Mr Robert Moss Collingham of Hessle, near Hull, and Henry Bolton of Hull, after a very pleasant visit to Nether Wasdale, arrived at

Wasdale Head by boat on the lake late in the evening and were glad to meet with the comfortable quarters and enjoy the hospitality of this house.

In 1761, in Nether Wasdale, was born Isaac Nicholson who was for ten years president of the Lady Huntingdon College at Chester. He died in 1807.

June 6.
J. M. Bottomley, Middlesbrough on Tees.
Robert Pearson, Helmsley, Yorkshire.
J. Arthur Slingsby, Ravenshaw, Skipton.
William Cecil Slingsby, Carleton, Skipton.
H. W. Pearson, Malton, Yorkshire.

John Barnard; Bryan and Margaret of London arrived June 6th and left June 7th. Everything as usual, very comfortable. Going to visit cairns.

June 9.
C. T. Tomlinson, Moss Side, Manchester.
F. L. Tomlinson.
Very comfortable and everything very clean.

June 17.
J. C. Waddington, Whalley.
J. A. Waddington, Burnley.
Fred W. Denny, Leeds.
H. I. Allison, Leeds.
James Brinley, all of Leicester.
Walter Brinley.
Edwin Brinley.
Also a hungry wayfarer, that we tumbled across at Scarf Gap and who was of some little service to us coming down Black Sail Pass. For which service, we asked him to take refreshment.

A merciful providence had fashioned him hollow,
On purpose he might the following swallow,
Which he did.

viz.
¾ of a quartern loaf
1 ¾ of cheese (Dutch)
½ lb butter
4 boiled eggs
1 quart ale

After partaking of this slight refreshment he borrowed one shilling off the landlady and 'shov'd'. It is to be hoped that a merciful providence will look after this young man's digestion, for he will stand greatly in need of it.

Black Sail Pass is the starting point for the ascent of both Pillar and

Steeple. These are two of the most popular climbs in the Lake District.

July 14.
Sarah J. Cockshutt, Ellermount, Kendal.
Florence and Alicia Swan, Edinburgh.
Emmeline and F. N. Cockshutt, Ellermount, Kendal.
July 13 to 14.
Mr. T. Whitaker, Birkenhead.
Mr. T. A. Whitaker, Birkenhead.
In every way well satisfied with the accommodation afforded.
July 15.
John J. Milligan, Kendal.
July 17.
H. P. Dempsey, Magd. College, Oxford.
A. F. Peterson, Christ Church College, Oxford.
W. O. Burrows, Christ Church College, Oxford.
July 18 to 20.
Annie Parr, Latham, Ormskirk.
Jessie Barry, Ormskirk.
William Parr, Ormskirk.
July 21.
Alfred North, Harbourne, Birmingham.
July 22.
T. H. Walrond, Balliol College, Oxford.
E. H. Railton, Snittlegarth.
July 23.
H. C. Montgomery and party, Belfast.
July 25.
Twas on a summer's evening; and the rain,
The benefits of whose persistent shower
My clothes from many a rightful place had borne,
Had ceased; and all my troubles had vamosed
Under the art of Mrs Tyson's hand.
With a clear sky, my evening stroll I took
And cogitated on my happy lot
When suddenly a vulgar, loud, guffaw
From shelter seeking tourists broke my dream
A single glance, the vision was dispelled
I turned and fled but not as fast as if
I had not carried Mr Tyson's clothes.

—Urban. P. Giles.

July 26.
J. C. Shurgarland, Hyde, near Manchester.
John Bradbury, Woodley, Nr Stockport.
July 27.
J. W. H. Allen, Anfield, Liverpool.

C. Sweeting, Dul. Univ.

George Freeman, Lombard Street, London.
F. Waymont, Croydon, Surrey.

Rev. R. T. Murray, Baltousboro' Parsonage, Glastonbury.
Mrs. Murray.
Miss Woodhouse, London.
July 28.
Thomas Sefton, Bolton le Moors.
Jos. Lightborn, Shrewsbury.
Found very comfortable lodgings.
July 29.
Robert Woodward, Storkholme, Worksop.
Clara Woodward.
July 30.
W. L. Hitchcock, Pembroke College, Cambridge and Whitburn Rectory, Sunderland.

H. M. Chataway, Emmanuel College, Cambridge and Peckleton, Leics.
W. S. Cherrington, St Johns College, Cambridge and Ipswich.
F. M. Lutyens, Trinity College, Cambridge and London.
Came from Keswick over Sty Head, July 30, returning via Buttermere July 31st.
Great Gable, so called from its shape, stands near Sty Head, between Scafell and Borrowdale.
August 1.
George Collinson, Halifax.
Francis Cumine, Birkenhead.
Thomas Collinson, Halifax.
August 2.
J. Molyneux-Jenkins, (CM) London.
T. Bullock (University of London), London.
Alfred Maxted, Newlands Grange, Ramsgate.

Mrs. Kidd, Liverpool.
Mrs. M. Soskry, and family, Liverpool.
Mrs. Blackie, St Bees.
Miss Perry, London.
Mrs. Bare, Liverpool.
Master W. Bare, Liverpool.
R. B. Ireland, Hensingham Lane, Whitehaven.

Edward S. Judd, London.
F. Maconachie, London.
August 3.
Walter Greenwood, Hull, Yorkshire.
James Gibson, Hull.
Arthur Jeff, Hull.

Alfred Bowman, after spending two very comfortable nights here, left for Buttermere.

Mannix and Whellan in 1847 wrote: 'The chapel of ease at Buttermere is a small plain building, with a bell-turret, re-built in 1841 at a cost of £300. The old chapel was perhaps the most diminutive in all England, being incapable of receiving more than half a dozen families within its walls.'

August 5.
Mr. and Mrs. Cordner, Sutherland.
Miss Paget.
August 7 to 11.
F. Barham, Carslake, Edgbaston.
L. B. Carslake, Clifton.
August 11.
Anne Joyce, Stockwell, London.
Hattie Geeves, Peterborough.
August 11 to 12.
M. Walls, Middlesex.
August 12.
G. C. Locket, Mill Hill, Hendon.
R. G. Gallop, Streatham, Surrey.
Well pleased and satisfied in every respect.

Lett----------, North Kensington, London.
August 13.
Isabel Piggot, Madingley, Twickenham.
Kate Atkins, Cambridge Park, Twickenham.
We would gladly stay a month.
August 14.
F. Sandford, St Johns College, Cambridge.
E. A. Gardner, Caius College, Cambridge.
R. B. Davies, St Johns College, Cambridge—Moor Court, Hington, Herefordshire.
August 2 to 15.
Rev. W. H. Fea, Whalley Range, Manchester.
H. R. Fea, Hull.
August 15.
Richard Wilton, Londesborough Rectory, East Yorkshire.
Cecil Wilton.

I. H. Etherington-Smith, Butharly Haw, Grasmere.
F. Peters Smith, St Michaels Nook, Grasmere.
August 17 to 18.
Charles Couchman, Henley in Arden.
Ernest H. Couchman, Rugby School and Balliol College.
Miss Short Semple, Balsall, Warwickshire.
Miss M. Short Semple, Balsall, Warwickshire.
A. H. Short, RMA, Woolwich.

From Borrowdale via Scawfell Pikes and Sty Head Pass to Buttermere via Black Sail and Scarf Gap.
J. H. S. McArthur, Ley School, Cambridge and London.
August 17 to 19.
P. P. - A. G. - J. H. - and G. W. McArthur came here via Scarf Gap and Black Sail Pass. Left for Coniston via Boot on 19th, after a pleasant stay.   •
At Boot, in the mid 19th century, there was a fair, held annually on September 2nd. A Provident Institution called the Independent Mechanics met at the King of Prussia Inn.

August 18 to 19.
Henry and Harold Glaisye, Birmingham and Brigham.
August 20.
Herbert Russell, Leicester.
James Harvey, Leicester.
H. P. Shadbolt, St Bartholomew's Hospital, London.
July 26 to 30, August 1 to 22.
Charles H. May, Pilgrim House, South Weald, Essex.
August 22.
Robert N. McBurney, New York, U.S.A.
Richard le Mort, New York, U.S.A.
August 23.
J. M. Pillams, Chislehurst.
G. Herbert Viccars, Leicester.
J. Sandys Stanyon, Leicester.
August 23 to 24.
J. J. Greenwood, Coventry.
W. G. Greenwood, Coventry.
August 24.
H. Mann, Leeds.

G. Y. Shuter, Dulhelm and Guys, London.
August 18 to 25.
J. B. Surgey, Brading, Isle of Wight.
Mr and Mrs Frederick Sheffield, Upper Norwood.

August 30.
Archdeacon Cooper.
Miss Violet Callender.
Rev. H. S. and Mrs. Callender.
C. B. Callender.
G. D. Callender.
Mrs. H. J. Dayrell Stowe and Miss Williams.
August 31.
Rev. Thomas Horsfall, Mexborough.
J. Ackroyd, Mexborough.

Miss Taylor, Alford, Lincs.

Miss Cartwright,   do
K. Butler,   do
Mabel Lanphier,   do
Edith Lanphier,   do
September 1.
C. Hastings, Silsden.
W. R. Hosking, all from Liverpool.
J. Hosking Jnr.
Edgar Hosking.
Josiah Hosking.
Charles R. Ashlin.

Miss Burkile, Scarborough.
Mrs. Sugden, Eastbourne.
September 4.
John Eastham, Southport.

Rev. R. Ewing, St Johns College, Oxford.
September 5.
Conrad Warner, Winchmore Hill.
Alice Warner, Hoddesdon, Herts.
Albert Fleming, Broxbourn, Herts.
T. W. Dougan, St Johns College, Cambridge.
September 3 to 6.
Kate Herbert, Tynemouth.
Constance Herbert, Gateshead.
J. A. Herbert, St Johns College, Cambridge.
E. W. Herbert, Gateshead.
September 6.
F. H. Hutton, Barnet.
W. Vincent, London.
September 7.
Alfred -----, Manchester.
A. E. Hughes, Manchester.
William Harrison, Manchester.
J. Beaumont Harrison, Manchester.
Ernest I. Everard, St Marks, Wolverhampton.
September 14.
H. Wilson, Southport.
F. Wilson, Southport.
September 13 to 15.
G. W. Blenkin, Trinity College, Cambridge.
L. S. Stanhope, New College, Oxford.
September 15.
M. Wells, Sale, Cheshire.
September 16.
Harry Williamson, Ashton on Mersey.
Joseph Todd, Birmingham.
Mr. Lawson, Seaton Carew.

Miss Lawson,   do
Miss M. Lawson, Seaton Carew.
September 15 to 17.
Mr. and Mrs. Joseph Toller, Kettering.
Jessie Gotch, Kettering.
Nellie Toller, Kettering.
T. N. Toller, Kettering.
September 17 to 18.
Mr. and Mrs. Forsham, Brook House, Fulwood, Preston.
Miss and Miss Lily Forsham,   do
Mr. C. H. Peart, Brook House, Fulwood, Preston.
Made exceedingly comfortable by hospitable Dame Tyson.
September 19
Arthur Pears, Putney.

September 27.
Ned Tucker, Woodlands, Ambleside.
October 16.
J. Dixon Butler, Redcliffe Gardens, London.
Stanley Howard, Woburn S, London.
From Ambleside via Rossett Gill, on to Keswick over Gable — a home from home.

F. Gardiner, Liverpool.
I. H ------, Manchester.
C. Picklington, Haydock.
L. Pilkington, Clifton.
E. Hulton, Manchester.
October 18.
Mrs. Thomas Woodley, Corfu.
Mr. and Mrs. Frederick Gardiner, Liverpool.
October 25 to 27.
Mr. and Mrs. W. Frederick Simpson, 53 Palace Gardens, Kensington, London.
November 1.
Tom Ledward, Victoria Park, Manchester.
W. Leonard Wills, Wild Green, Birmingham.
November 13.
W. Ainslie and H. R. King, Windermere.
December 29.
F. E. Wilson, Macclesfield.
Claude Wilson, Edinburgh.
Professor John Wilson, the eminent critic, essayist and poet, better known as 'Christopher North', made his home at Elleray, Windermere in 1807. He was a member of Wordsworth's circle and a visitor to Row Farm.

1882

March 28 to April 4.
A. A. Ethelston, Christ Church College, Oxford.
April 7.
Good Friday, glorious fine day.
Miles Bell, Liverpool.
James Gray, Youghal, County Cork.
Robert L. Gray, County Cork.
Thomas Jennings, Caldbeck.
W. Lute, Claughton.
E. J. Preston, St Johns, London.
W. J. Preston, St Johns, London.
Denton describes Caldbeck as being 'a dale lying between Warnell Fell and the mountains, Carrick and Grisdale Fells.'

March 22 to April 7.
A. F. Peterson, Christ Church College, Oxford.
A. L. Mumm, C. C. C., Oxford.
April 8.
Eustace Hulton, Manchester.
A. E. Craven, London.
J. H. Hulton, Bolton.
James Heelis, Manchester.

Thomas Tebbutt, Manchester.
Edward Shaw, Liverpool.
Daniel Rea, Liverpool.
Alice Rea, Eskdale.
April 9.
M. H. Peacock MA., Exeter College, Oxford.
T. P. Peacock, Leeds.
I. H. Potter, Leeds.

A. Sweeting, Liverpool.
E. Ludcke (B.A., London), Liverpool.
R. J. Lloyd (B.A., London), Liverpool.
April 10.
John Redhead, Barrow in Furness.
W. Gordon, Barrow in Furness.

J. S. Twyford, Liverpool.
W. M. Pendlebury, Liverpool.
The population of Barrow in 1847 was 325. By 1864 it had increased to 10,608 and in 1891 was 51,712. This extraordinary prosperity was due to the abundance of rich hematite ore which in the 19th century converted a fishing hamlet into one of the most important centres of iron manufacture in the world.

April 11.
Edward Cumberlage.
B. H. Barrington, Keswick.
April 12.
J. W. Allen, Liverpool.
A. Hawkings, Liverpool.
A. S. Vingoe, Liverpool.
March 22 to April 13.
C. Cannan and H. R. King.
April 17.
C. M. March, Leeds.
G. E. Du Croz, Weybridge.
C. L. B. Elliott, Henbury.
William H. Wardle, Ednaston Lodge, Near Derby.
April 20.
Herbert Wilson, Stratford on Avon.
Claud Wilson, Edinburgh.
April 21 to 23.
W. A. Waddington, Burnley.
J. A. Waddington, Burnley.
May 15.
H. Strong, Lordship Park, London.
May 18.
Samuel Walker, Irwell, Bury.
Miss M. C. Walker, Bury.
May 21.
C. Hopkinson, Manchester.
May 22.
Patrick Cowan, Maryport.
Robert R. Cowan, Maryport.
William Hardcastle, Gateshead.
May 24.
A. I. Stretton, Brockley, Kent.
W. S. B. Stretton, Brockley.
F. G. Stretton, Brockley.

Ho ye who seek a sure relief
To ease the troubled brain
And ye who spend a life of grief
A daily search for gain

Remember life is but a span
At best a troubled dream
So sleep a little when you can
Beside a mountain stream
There is a bracing air that blows
On Scawfell's gloomy height
There is a peaceful stream that flows
Through Wastdale's valley bright
Then haste ye! Haste! To Wastdale fair
To quit the busy din
There is new life in mountain air
A refuge safe from sin.

May 28.
Grace Drew, London.
Christabel Drew, London.
G. H. Drew, London.
From Langdale on the 27th, left today for Buttermere.
May 29.
William McSt-----, Sunderland.
George Barnes, Sunderland.
Henry Horner, Sunderland.
John Young, Sunderland.
John Parker, Sunderland.
Robert Richards, Sunderland.

John G. Allen, Formby.
W. E. Corrie, 4 Kingsmount, Birkenhead.
May 30.
George Sturrock, Bradford.
Hogo Wagner, Crinmitzchaz.

John C. Walker, Manchester.
Geoffrey A. Solly.
May 31.
I. H. Etherington-Smith, Butharlyp Howe, Grasmere.
F. Peters-Smith, St Michaels Nook, Grasmere.

Thomas Crofton (pater), South Shields.
Mrs. Hornby Crofton.
James Coburn Crofton, son of the above Thomas.
George Hudson Crofton, son of the above Thomas.

Burdett Sellers, Preston.
Thomas D. Sellers, Preston.
June 1.
H. J. Lees, Nottingham.
Louis Bircumshaw, Nottingham.

Edward Ash, Nottingham.

Sprinkling Tarn Camp:-
William Bell, Manchester and Ambleside.
Charles Bell, Manchester and Ambleside.
B. Schofield, Huddersfield.
W. E. Percival, Ambleside.

N. Bell, Ambleside.
William Monkhouse, Manchester.
Edward Tucker, Elterwater, Ambleside.
June 3.
Isaac Grundy, Bolton le Moors.
M. Crompton, Bolton le Moors.
Jonathan Brookes, Manchester.
Ernest A. Brookes, Manchester.
Started from Keswick 9 a.m., arrived at Buttermere via Borrowdale
and Honister Pass; lunched and then proceeded at 2.15 p.m., to
Wastwater via Scarf Gap on Black Sail Passes; where we arrived at
5.15 drenched to the skin and were very cordially received by the
hostess of this hotel, who provided us with the 'maister's' breeks
and duds generally. Start for Ambleside via Scawfell tomorrow
8 a.m.
June 1 to 9.
Mr. and Mrs. Reginald Lake, Watford.

George Reade, London.
I. H. A. Paley Reade, London.
June 9.
J. Hamilton Gair, Liverpool.
June 10.
Wem gottwill rechte Gunst erweisen,
Den schickt er in die weite Welt.
Dem will er seine Wunder weisen
In Berg und Thal und Strom und Feld.
Ueberall bin ich zu Hause,
Ueverall werd ich vekannt.
Macht mein Reisen im Norden Pause,
Wird der Sud, der west oder ost mein Vaterland.
—Louis Bancks, Magdeburg, Germany.

June 12.
Miss Whetham, London.
Miss Stovell, London.
June 16.
Mrs. Walker, Borrowdale Vicarage.
Mrs. Richardson, St Leonards.
Mrs. Tyson gave us an excellent tea, started on our return walk to
Borrowdale Vicarage at 5.p.m.

William Gilpin wrote in 1772, 'This valley, so replete with hideous grandeur, is known by the name of the straits of Borrowdale.'

June 19.
William Driver.
Mrs. and Miss Driver, Market Harborough.
June 20.
Alfred Larder, 11 Scotts Street, Hull.
Thomas Sadler, Eastbourne Street, Hull.
Arrived here at 8.p.m., after a long and fatiguing walk from Coniston via Tilberthwaite Fell Foot, Boot and Burnmoor Tarn. Roads very rough. A substantial tea was provided by Mrs. Tyson in a few minutes, which, seeing that we had breakfasted at 7.30. a.m., and had had very little in the meantime, we thoroughly enjoyed it.
There are, on the shores of Coniston Water, several bloomery sites, where iron ore was smelted. Vast amounts of charcoal were needed for the process and these were obtained from coppices in the area. The ore was brought up the River Crake.

June 22.
A. F. Williams, St Johns College and New Zealand.
H. W. Williams, Jesus College, Cambridge.
June 26.
Mr. and Mrs. I. R. Dowthwaite, London.
June 27.
G. H. P. Joy, Leeds.
Mr. and Mrs. George O. Joy, Leeds.
June 28.
Rev. H. and Mrs. Leigh Mallory, Cambridge.
June 29.
A. E. Lankester, The Stricklands, Stowmarket.
Ernest H. Lankester,   do
Frank Lankester,   do
June 30.
W. A. Raleigh, Kings College, Cambridge.
I. G. L. Welldon, Kings College, Cambridge.
C. F. Clay, Trinity College, Cambridge.
C. C. Mead, Cambridge.
July 5.
Samuel Watkinson, Hull.
Josiah Watkinson, University College, London and York.
July 6.
John H. Binns, Bradford.
A. E. Binns, Bradford.
C. A. Binns, Bradford.

From Keswick Town by Borrowdale
Three sturdy brothers came.
But soon Scarf Gap and steep Black Sail

These sturdy spirits tame
The plummet line is pretty straight
Likewise the arrows tracks
But nought can 'tak a straighter gate'.
Than the rain did down our backs.

July 7.
Rev. H. Lonsdale, Thornwaite Vicarage.
W. Windley, Trinity College, Cambridge.
Alice Rea, Eskdale.
Hope Rea, Eskdale.
R. M. Rea, Liverpool.
James H. Rea, Liverpool.
J. Markland, Ramsbottom, Bury.

The Ravenglass and Eskdale Railway, known locally as 'La'al Ratty', is a major tourist attraction. It started life in 1875 for the transportation of iron ore. Passengers were first carried in 1876 and this 15inch gauge railway has the right to carry Her Majesty's Mail and issue stamps.

July 10.
F. S. Copleston, ------------

July 11.
Mr. and Mrs. Northey, St Leonards.
F. Northey, Hastings.
Rev. E. G. Copleston, Wokingham.
July 12.
John Ferguson, Maryport.
James Frier, Galashiels.
Walter Charles Chappel, Sunderland.
July 15.
Edward Faithern, Ch. Chu., Albany Street.
Most comfortable.
July 18.
Miss Wallis, Basinstoke, Hampshire.
Miss S. J. Wallis.
R. Sterry Wallis.
July 18 to 19.
James M. Nicol, Leeds.
H. Illingworth Allison, Selby (fourth visit).
July 20.
William Nuttall, Bradford.
H. Coward, Sheffield.

Thomas Rose Jnr. Brighton.
John George Upperby, London Hospital and S. Africa.
R. W. Leadbeater, Scarborough.
E. B. Morrin, North Shields.

A. Morrin.
John Morrin Jnr.
July 21.
Urban P. Giles, 76 St Pauls Road, Canonbury, London (third visit).
July 26.
J. W. C. Atkinson, Manningham, Bradford.
Richard Pawson,   do
J. W. Gregory, Clapton, London.
July 29 to 31.
Paul Greenwood, Leeds.
George Nicholson, Leeds.
August 1.
Walter Greenwood, Hull.
Richard H. Jeff, Hull.
July 13 to August 2.
H. B. Simpson, Magdalen College, Oxford.

August 3.
Rev. W. Chaplin, Vicar of Stavely.
William Chaplin Jnr, Stavely.
Miss N. Chaplin.
Miss I. Canning, London.
I. H. Boyd Thomson, Stavely.
Alfred Tyson, Stavely.
August 4.
Charles Donkin Jnr, Sunderland.
From Keswick via Sty Head.

T. W. Hardy, and Miss Hardy.

F. E. Green, Old Charlton.
Emma Green, Brighton.
Margarat Beck, Cheam, Surrey.
August 5 to 6.
R. W. Cameron, Owens College, Manchester.
Jonathan Watson, Southport.
August 7.
A. H. Dawson, Crosshills, Leeds.
I. Smith,   do
Alex Kemp, Crosshills, Leeds.
Arthur H------,   do

Thomas Watts, Leicester.
G. Tempest Wade, Belgrave.
August 8.
Mrs. and Miss Norris, Bramhall, Cheshire.
Henry Lawson, Liverpool.

Joseph Mason, Leeds.

The hazards of rock climbing, as seen by guests at Row Farm on August 3rd, 1880, who added this sketch to the visitors' books.

For the goodness of her Hyson
We must praise Mrs Tyson

Charles Stephenson

Harold Hebblethwaite. B.N.S. Y.N. Union. B.G.S.C.C.
James Robert Thackrah. Halifax.
Wm. H. Hatch, Halifax

View of the Scawfell Range

Are these the Likes
of Scawfell Pikes

More sketches in the visitors' books on August 10th, 1880. As with other illustrations, the humour is of the heavy Victorian variety. The lower drawing carries the legend: 'Are these the Likes of Scawfell Pikes.'

A holiday excursion in the Wasdale area. It was sedate and no doubt more than slightly uncomfortable outings of this kind that brought many day visitors to Row Farm.

A Wasdale classroom, photographed at about the period covered by this book.

Changing ways of crossing Sty Head Pass, the important route connecting Wasdale with Borrowdale at an altitude of 1,600 feet. Top: A traveller in the age of deference complete with pack pony and guide. Bottom: A present-day walker with pack on her back contemplates the climb up the pass from the Wasdale side. (Tom Parker).

Opposite: The summit of Sty Head Pass, with Wasdale on the left, Great Gable dominant in the centre and Sty Head Tarn at its foot. (Leonard & Marjorie Gayton).

Many of the visitors to Row Farm walked over from Buttermere for tea, regarding the six-mile walk with its climbs of the 1,200 ft Scarth (or Scarf) Gap Pass and 1,800 ft Black Sail Pass as an afternoon stroll. After tea they walked back again! This view from Green Gable shows part of the route they took, with Black Sail (left) and Scarth Gap (right) separated by the upper reaches of Ennerdale. (Leonard & Marjorie Gayton).

Aug. 28th. R. S. Kindersley
H R King } windrummen.

Aug 28th J. F. Caröe From Lows Wood over the Pikes but only
Saw the Cairn on the lee side.
W D Caröe. N.B. Prefer slower baths at home.
J. O. C. London.
Aug. 28. J. N. Lawton Heyrod Stalybridge

Aug.st 31st 1882
Arthur Shaw Taylor Hill
Huddersfield

Fredk Hy Green
Kilburn, London.

Aug 30th 1882 George Wakefield
Stretford
Wm Manchester

John Hancock Shelford, Mr/tr.

There four came from Keswick over Styhead The day was all
that could be desired & the Vale of Borrowdale was
truly lovely & Styhed grand

Aug 31st / 82 J R Thompson } W har
J H Muncaster

Aug of Sept R W Cameron Owbar Coll. Manchester.

Sept 15/82   Mr & Mrs T. S. Townend ⎱ London
             Mr & Mrs. Stoker   ⎰
             Mr T. Dunning

Sept 17/82   Mr F. W. Lockwood   Hon Sec. Belfast Naturalists' Field Club

   "   R. H. Lockwood.   Kendal.
Sep 20th/82 J. O. Morgan   Sydenham

Sept 21st   Arthur Foster Esqr.
             Miss Foster   Bath
             Captn. C. E. Davis.   Bath

Sept 22nd   Henry Coulter   London
             Ewald Willson.

Mr Wilson and his venerable friend above named have
had a short but very enjoyable experience of Wastdale, and of the
comforts of this very comfortable house and of the attention &
courtesy of their hostess — May her shadow never grow less!

September 25th   Mr C. Innes & Miss Innes   London

Oct 2nd   — Mrs Marsland Hopkins   ⎱
             Miss Magdalen K. Hopkins.   ⎰ Oxford.
             C. B. Hopkins.
             Miss G. H. Hopkins,
             Rev A. L. Cummeline, Magd. Coll. Oxford

We were made very comfortable during the two days we stayed, and
wish particularly to record our gratitude for the dry clothes lent to us
when we arrived wet through from Borrowdale   also the next day from
Black Sail   "High he! the wind & the rain"
             "The rain it raineth every day"

                              4th Oct 1882.

Entries in the Visitors' Books for August and September 1882. The references to the wet
weather are, as might be expected, typical.

The matchless view from Westmorland Cairn on Great Gable, with the patchwork quilt of Wasdale stretching away to Wastwater and its famous screes. (Tom Parker).

George Poxson, Leeds.
Walter Ingleson, Leeds.
August 10.
William Bradfield, Fox Grove, Kingsclere.
August 11.
There is a way of climbing the Pillar Rock starting from the Eastern side and coming up the Ennerdale face above Low Man. Quitting the neck which joins the rock to the mountain, and on the eastern side of the rock passing the beginning of the 'easy way', descend the gully as far as you can, to where the great chimney runs straight up to the summit. (This is the chimney in whose top the 'easy way' with the grass slope ends.)

Climb this, keeping the wall on the right to about 20 feet from the perpendicular rock, then get out on the right and cross the low wall of rock. Work round to the left on the grass, keeping well under the main rock. Low Man is in front of you, rather to the right. After about 50 feet you come to a small triangular grass slope with a deep chimney at the top, about 12 feet high. Climb this: or you may go round it outside over the sloping rocks. On reaching the top of the chimney, do not go up the grass, but climb the cliff by the first chimney on the left, and then go up the grass steps of a second chimney to a large cubical block, which seems to stand loose on a projecting corner. In front of you, on the right, you will see a vertical cleft with a step in the middle. Climb this and scramble to the top as you please. Though longer than the 'easy way', it is not difficult with care and a good fair climb from end to end.

Walter Parry Haskett-Smith.
F. H. Bowring.
J. A. Hamilton.
W. Bartlett.

August 9 and 12.
Mickledore is so well known to climbers, that many may be glad to hear of an alternative route up these glorious crags, which, while less hackneyed, than the 'Split Rock' and 'Broad Stand' way, has not the danger of the Penrith men's climb from the 'Rake's Progress' on the right! The gully on the Eskdale side, perhaps hardly admits of being climbed direct to the top and it is therefore necessary to emerge to the right and this can hardly be done too early. Looking back after an ascent of some 30 feet of gully and stepping up on to a low ledge on the Eskdale side, a broad ledge will be observed below you on the opposite wall!

This ledge is reached by clinging to the wall and shifting carefully along and from it a good spring will land you on flat grass! The ledge may be also reached from the very foot of the gully by taking to the rock at once by the corner and working round to the left. The rest is simple enough, keep up with the gully well on the left and return into it above the sudden pitch, which occurs about half way on it. You will soon come to a mossy chimney, on emerging through

which, you will find yourself at the top, close to the grand chasm of 'Deep Ghyll'.
Walter Parry Haskett-Smith.

August 12.
Climbed the face of Lingmell Crags to the cairn from Piers Ghyll.
Walter Parry Haskett-Smith.
J.A. Hamilton.
July 18 to August 14.
J.A. Hamilton, Balliol College, Oxford.
W.P. Haskett-Smith, Trinity College, Oxford.
W. Bartlett, C.C.C., Oxford.
W.E. Bowen, Balliol College, Oxford.

Walter Parry Haskett-Smith, later to be recognised throughout the world as the 'Father of British Climbing', came to Wasdale Head for the first time in 1881 as a member of a University Reading Party. He was then 22 years old. At Row Farm he met F.H. Bowring, then in his sixties and an enthusiastic and knowledgeable hill walker, who introduced Haskett-Smith to the challenging sport of rock climbing.

Bowring, a Fellow of Trinity College, was a native of the West Country. Although in his sixties he walked with a splendid swing and climbed with great vigour and precision. It was he who introduced Haskett-Smith to John Wilson Robinson of Lorton, Cockermouth. Haskett-Smith and Robinson were to make one of the finest rock-climbing teams ever known in the Lake District.

Educated at Eton, W.P. Haskett-Smith went on to Trinity College, Oxford. In 1880 he obtained a degree in Classic Moderations. The following year, Haskett-Smith was reading for a degree in Literae Humaniores. Two years later he passed with honours. His first visit to the Tysons and the Lake District lasted a month. In 1882, Haskett-Smith returned to begin rock-climbing in earnest. He sought out all the gullies and ridges that seemed to offer reasonable routes and climbed as many as he could. Of 20 new climbs discovered in the Wasdale area, all but three were climbed by Haskett-Smith and in most cases he climbed them alone.

He was the pioneer of the very earliest routes on a number of different Lakeland crags. It was he who first discovered and climbed Napes Needle in 1886 and did it solo. Fifty years later when 74, this remarkable man celebrated the anniversary by climbing Napes Needle once more. The climb took place on Easter Saturday. Haskett-Smith was led up to the summit by Lord Chorley, then president of the Fell and Rock Club, before an admiring audience of many hundreds, ranged round the Dress Circle, the rocky bag on the Napes from which the Needle stands out. Walter Parry Haskett-Smith also climbed extensively in the Alps, the Pyrenees, North Africa, the Balkans, the Andes, in Norway and the Rockies. However, it was on climbing in the Lake District, that he left his most permanent mark. A bachelor, he died in 1946 in Dorset.

August 14.
The Rev. I. Grosvenor Morris, Cardiff College.
George B. Hughes, Cardiff College.
Robert L. Rees, Cheshire.
W.J. Roderick Rees, Cheshire.
George A. Havelock, Newcastle upon Tyne.
J.B. Clark, Newcastle upon Tyne.
Raymond St George Ross, Manchester.
Gilbert Middleton, Fairfield, Leeds.
F.H. Pinchers, Wakefield.
J.B. Cooke, Wakefield.
August 14 to 16.
T. Walls, and all from Middlesex.
August 16 to 17.
Captain Burrows, R.N., Oxford.
Miss Burrows, Oxford.
Miss Gardiner, Oxford.
E.H. Burrows, Devon.
August 17.
J.H.E---------, Birmingham.
August 18 to 19.
J.F. Longrigg, Queens College, Oxford.
H.S. Wood,   do
J.B. Hewestson,   do
August 19.
George Sayer, Pett Place, Charing, Kent.
Mr., Mrs. and the Misses Ward, London.
Mr. and Mrs. F. Peterson Ward, 46 Hamilton Terrace, St Johns Wood, London.
The Misses F. Peterson Ward.
August 18 to 21.
M. Mercer-Adam, London.
C. Mortlock, London.
H. Mortlock, London.
Isaac Hall, Edge Lane, Liverpool.
John Wesley wrote in April 1761: 'We were soon lost in the mountains; but in an hour we found a cottage and a good woman who bade her son "take the galloway and guide them to the fell foot". There we met a poor man. He piloted us over the next mountain, the like to which, I never beheld either in Wales or Germany. As were were climbing the third, a man overtook us, who was going the same road; so he accompanied us till we were in a plain level way which in three hours brought us to Whitehaven.'
It is considered opinion that Wesley took the route from Ambleside by Wrynose and Hardknott to Eskdale, then over Burnmoor, with Scafell on his right down to Wasdale and then by Black Sail Pass into Ennerdale, where he would soon be on a plain level way to

115

*Whitehaven. If this was so, then John Wesley was the first person
to travel through the central Lakeland passes and leave an account
of his journey.*
August 21.
James B. Hewitt, 11 Binns Road, Edge Lane, Liverpool.
August 22 to 23.
Arthur R. Reed, Sunderland.
Arthur Peters, Sunderland.
'Ho! everyone that thirsteth'

A.H. Leaky, Woolwich.
Miss Leaky, Woolwich.
August 25.
Rev. E.A. Brown, Burnage Rectory, Manchester.
Mrs Brown.
Mr. W.T. Baldey, Southsea.

W.R. Metcalfe, Malton, Yorkshire.
T. Carter Clough, Malton.
August 26.
Started from Keswick at 9.30 — walked by Newlands to Buttermere —
thence to Scale Force, which we saw in spendid form — climbed by
Gale Fell and Red Pike, thence to High Style and High Crag.
Saw some grand effects of mist in Ennerdale and on the face of the
Pillar Mountain, while the sun was bright in Buttermere and
Derwentwater. Crossed head of Ennerdale and over Black Sail to
Wasdale, where we were greeted by the wanted rain, and the no less
wanted kindness of Mrs Tyson. Off this morning to Whitehaven
by the Pillar and Ennerdale Lake.
James A.H. Murray, LLD., Mill Hill, London.
Harold J. Ruthven Murray, 14 years.
Wilfred G. Ruthven Murray, 10 years.

Phillip H. Wickstead, London.
Ewing R. Wickstead, London.

George Watson Gray, 106 Princess Consort Road, Gateshead on
Tyne.

Jumbo says to Alice, I love you — Alice says to
Jumbo, I don't believe you,
If you love me truly, as you say you do
You would not go to yankee land and leave me in the zoo.
August 28.
R.S. Kindersley, Windermere.
H.R. King, Windermere.

J. F. Caroe, From Lowood over the Pikes, but only saw the cairn on

116

the lee side.
W.D. Caroe, J.O.C. London.
N.B. Prefer showerbathes at home.

I.N. Lorton, Stalybridge.
August 30.
Arthur Shaw, Taylot Hill, Huddersfield.
Frederick Henry Green, Kilburn, London.
George Wakefield, Stretford, Manchester.
John Hancock, Stretford, Manchester.
These four came from Keswick over Sty Head. The day was all that could be desired and the Vale of Borrowdale was truly lovely and Sty Head grand.
August 31.
J.R. Thompson, Whitehaven.
J.H. Muncaster, Whitehaven.

August 27 to September 3.
R.W. Cameron, Owens College, Manchester.
September 3.
J.E. Hogg, Hemel Hempstead.
September 5.
Miss Aitcheson, Wallsend on Tyne.
Miss H. Aitcheson, Wallsend.

Mr. and Mrs. H. Parker, Ceylon.

R. St John Ainslie, Oriel College, Oxford.
W. Ainslie, Windermere.

C.S. Joy, St Peters College, Cambridge.
P.C. Joy, Winchester College.
September 7.
Mr. and Mrs. A.H. Eddington, Kendal.
Miss Short, Darlington.
September 8.
Mr. and Mrs. H.A. Elevach, Mill Hill, London.

Mr. and Mrs. Rowland Venables, Old Colwall, Malvern.

W.J. Walkington.
A.H. Gardner.
D.C. Guirron.
Arrived at Dame Tyson's after a tedious journey across Scarff Gap and Black Sail Pass from Crummock Water. Thankful to arrive at a hospitable house.
The fishing at Buttermere, in 1439, was worth 6s 8d. Crummock, which was 26s 8d, was let by Peter Johnson in the same year. In 1480 it was let to William Pereson, or as he is called a few lines

after, in the Percy Records, 'William Pereson Johnson is the tenant.'
Obviously he was the first man's son. This was an instance of how
'son' surnames could be fluid, even in the 15th century.

September 9.
Robert A. Sloan, Birkenhead.
G. Wallace, Birkenhead.
Jon Caird, Birkenhead.
September 7 to 9.
H. J. Roby, Manchester.
F. H. Roby, Manchester.
September 8 to 10.
Josiah Hoskings, Liverpool.
Edith Hoskings.
Edgar Hoskings.
Josiah Hoskings, Jnr.
September 9 to 10.
Arthur Young, London.
William G. Gardner, London.
September 11.
J. R. Wynne Edwards, Carlisle.
H. C. Wynne Edwards, Denbigh.

George Warrener, Darlington.
Jonathan H. Waites, Darlington.
September 12 to 13.
I. P. Mulcaster, Benwell.
Charlotte A. Mulcaster, Benwell.
W. V. Mulcaster, Benwell.
September 12.
Tom W. Benson, Halifax.
T. W. Fawthrup, Halifax.
September 15.
Mr. and Mrs. Horatio Pennington and Mr. Arthur Pennington
leaving after a pleasant little visit—during a little rain, tea, roses
and honeydew make the visit very comfortable with the kind
attention we received. We hope to come again.
July 20 to September 4, September 9 to 16.
F. H. Bowring, Lincolns Inn, London.
September 15.
Mr. and Mrs. T. P. Townend, London.
Mr. and Mrs Stoker, London.
Mr. T. Dunning, London.
September 17.
Mr. F. W. Lockwood, Belfast Naturalist Field Club.
P. H. Lockwood, Kendal.
September 20.
T. D. Morgan, Sydenham.

September 21.
Arthur Foster, Bath.
Miss Foster, Bath.
Mrs. C. E. Davis, Bath.

September 22.
Henry Coulter, London.
Gerald Willson, Haverstock Hill, London.
Mr. Willson and his venerable friend above named, have had a short, but very enjoyable experience of Wasdale, and of the comforts of this very comfortable house and of the attention and courtesy of their hostess. May her shadow never grow less!
In 1811, it is recorded about Wasdale Head chapel, that 'no burials are at it.' They had to go 20 miles to the mother church of St Bees for interments.

September 25.
Mr. C. Innes, London.
Miss Innes, London.

October 2.
Mrs. Marsland Hopkins, Oxford.
Miss Magdalen K. Hopkins, Oxford.
C. B. Hopkins, Oxford.
Miss G. F. M. Hopkins, Oxford.
Rev. A. S. Commeline, Magd. College, Oxford.
We were made very comfortable during the two days we stayed, and wish particularly to record our gratitude for the dry clothes lent to us when we arrived wet through from Borrowdale—also the next day from Black Sail.
'Heigh Ho! the wind and the rain'
'The rain it raineth every day'.

October 4.
Mrs. Shaw, Stockwell, London.
Miss Shaw, London.
Very comfortable advise all to take up quarters at Dame Tyson's hospitable roof.

October 5.
Mr. and Mrs. C. J. Goodman, London.

October 12/13.
J. Maitland, London.
D. C. Reed, London.
L. B. Maitland, London.
December 26 to 28.
H. Woolley, Manchester.
R. J. Cheshire, Manchester.

1883

January 5 to 6.
Arthur J. Grant, Kings College, Cambridge.
W. White, Boston, Lincs.
Saw some very perfect fog-bows on Scawfell.
Scafell looks down on Wasdale Head, whose tiny church is one of the smallest in England. The east window is in memory of 'the happy and prosperous reign of Her Majesty Queen Victoria.'

February 15.
Edward Rathbone, Liverpool.
March 23 to 25.
I. W. H. Thorp, Macclesfield.
E. C. Kendall, Liverpool.
March 26.
J. W. H. Thorp, Macclesfield.
E. C. Kendall, Chester.
March 28 to 30.
John Mason M.B., St Bartholomews Hospital, London.
April 6.
Thomas Tyson, Whitehaven.
John Edward Tyson, Whitehaven.
Thomas Bailey Tyson, Whitehaven.
Came over from Boot on the 4th, over the fells by Burnmmor Tarn.
March 14 to April 9.
A. F. Peterson, Christ Church College, Oxford.
A. L. Mumm, Christ Church College, Oxford.
C. Cannan, Lincoln College, Oxford.
J. E. King, Lincoln College, Oxford.
H. R. King, Lincoln College, Oxford.
April 26.
Rev. G. J. Hall, Shrewsbury.
Edw. B. Moser, Shrewsbury.
April 30.
H. R. Woolsych, Rossall.
J. R. White, Rossall.
W. M. Baker, Rossall.
W. King, Rossall.

May 11.
H. W. Smith (Aylesbury, Bucks), Bromley, Kent.
W. R. Adams, Croydon.
R. de M. Rudolf, Clapham.
May 14.
A. H. Arkle, Oxton.
C. A. Arkle, Birkenhead.
From Keswick via Honister, Scarf Gap and Black Sail pass.

R. McMurray, Whitehaven.
May 15.
Franklin Hurst, Westminster and Sale, Cheshire.
J. R. Leach, Didsbury and Manchester.
May 18.
A. W. Upcott, Westminster School.
J. J. Malloch, Swanton Novess, Norfolk.
May 19.
J. M. Bell, Liverpool.

Isaac Chorlton, Withington, Manchester.
William Lincoln, London.
May 21.
Walter D. May, Prinswick, Gloucester.

Fanny M. Forester, Kircaldy.
In hopes of returning another summer to see Mrs. Tyson and enjoy
her hospitality.
H. P. Dempsey, Wallasey, Cheshire.
H. B. Dempsey.

There was a sound of revelry by day,
For two Carthusians had gathered there
From Borrowdale they'd come and wished to stay
To get some lunch at Dame Tyson's and when
They'd eaten quite enough for twenty men
They started, and to Buttermere did go
And one of them not having any pen
With a lead pencil wrote this stanza so
And then away they went as straight as flies the crow.
St James Church at Buttermere was built in 1840. The east window
depicting Martha was installed in 1893 and is by Henry Holliday
(1839-1927).

May 22.
The Hon. Lady Inglis.
Miss Victoria Inglis.
Miss Julia Inglis.
May 26.
Mrs H. S. Walker, Borrowdale Vicarage.

Mrs. Miller and Miss Whitehead, Werndee Hall, South Norwood. *At the south end of Derwentwater is the bridge, often painted by artists; it leads to the village of Grange-in-Borrowdale, a place mentioned many times in the Herries stories by Sir Hugh Walpole (1884-1941).*

May 30.
C. E. Harrison, Bradford, Yorks.
Emily Harrison, Bradford, Yorks.
May 31.
C. Entwiste, Studley, Warwickshire.
B. Entwiste, Wolhayes, Christ Church, Hants.
June 4.
Rev. Harold H. Wright, Parish Church, Scarborough.
John Storer, Mus Bac; Oxon; Parish Church, Scarborough.

We started on Monday, May 28th from Scarborough by rail to Penrith. We then walked round by Beacon Hill, Brougham Castle, Mayborough to Pooley. Next day Tuesday, we walked from Pooley to Patterdale calling on Aira Force by the way, and ascending Place Fell when we got there. On Wednesday we crossed over Helvellyn by Striding Edge on to Keswick. Thursday ascended Skiddaw and visited all the attractions in the neighbourhood of Keswick. Friday walked from Keswick through Borrowdale by Honister Pass to Buttermere. Saturday ascended Robinson and visited Scale Force and rested there on the Sunday. Monday, June 4th, walked from Buttermere by the Scarf Gap and Black Sail Pass to WASTDALE HEAD and ascended the Screes. Today June 5th, we proceed onwards to Dungeon Ghyll over Scawfell Pike.
Known at Wasdale Head as 'Down in the Dale Bridge', the old pack-horse bridge has been widened slightly to take cars.

June 8.
Mr. and Mrs. Wilson, Maryport.

W. Marshall, Balham, S. W. London.

C. Barker, Hornsey, Ryde.

Bert Thompson, Keswick.

W. Marshall, Dublin.
C. A. Langston, Dublin.

Mrs. Thompson, Borrowdale.
June 12.
W. Hay Fea, Cottingham, Yorkshire.
H. R. Fea, Cottingham.

Mr. and Mrs. J. Forsham, Brook House, Fulwood, Preston.

Mrs. and Miss Lily Forsham.
Mr. C. H. Plant, Preston.
From Coniston via Burnmoor en route to Buttermere.

Mr. and Miss Thom, Aberdeen.

Miss Emily Hyde, Stratford on Avon.
Miss E. Stuart, Stratford on Avon.
Lorton Hall in the village of Lorton, near to Buttermere, has a pele tower, haunted by the ghost of a woman who walks with a lighted candle. There are also two priest-holes in the Hall.

June 13 to 16.
John Martin, Hull.
James Gibson, Hull.
June 16.
Mary Bell, Ambleside.
Annie Bell, Ambleside.
Margaret Bell, Ambleside.
Charles Bell,   do
June 15th: From Ambleside to Wastdale Head via Scawfell Pike.
June 16th: On to Seascale via Gosforth.
The church of St Cuthbert at Seascale has a clock on the west front which commemorates the coronation of King George VI in 1937.

June 16.
Mr. and Mrs. Botterill, Eppleworth Grange, Cottingham.
Mr. and Mrs. I. C. Barker, Hull.
June 21.
W. R. Corrie, Birkenhead.
From Ambleside to here for a week.
June 24.
John G. Allen, Formby.
June 23 to 30.
C. F. Clay, Trinity College, Cambridge.
C. C. Mead, Cambridge.
Second Visit.
June 25 to 30.
H. McLeod Innes, Trinity College, Cambridge.

Mr Clay (B.A.)
Went one day
For to catch some fish
But when he got there
The beck was bare
And so the poor dog got none.
July 3.
W. M. Dingwall, Trinity College, Cambridge.
H. G. Gwinner, Trinity College, Cambridge.

These (Universal) boys from here,
By Jove and Juno swore,
O'er Scawfell's rugged Pikes to go
Till Dungeon Ghyll they saw,
By Jove and Juno swore it,
But found a misty day,
In cloud and darkness on they pressed
North and south and east and west
For they had lost their way.

North and south and east and west
They turned with footsteps slow,
Till down a long and rugged Ghyll
They spied a house below.
But shame! Those fools had only got
Back to Dame Tyson's door;
Where whiskey hot, dry shoes, and socks,
And borrowed bags they wore.

July 5.
Lewis Rendel, 8 Rutland Gate, London.
July 6.
Full pleasant I ween, when a fellow had been
Tramping all day by crag, beck, and ravine,
Tired and thirsty, and not over clean,
Longing in vain for the vintage of Burton,
(With the night coming on, of the road not quite certain).
At last to behold far away oer the wolde
A light beaming bright through the night mist so cold.
Soon after he's sipping his 'Congo' or 'Hyson'
At the clean, cosy hostel of good Dame Tyson.
Then the softest of couches invites his repose;
He his lullaby owes, to the streamlet which flows
Near his window and drowsily sings as it goes
In a way that would make even Cerberus doze;
And strange though it seems, it fills all his dreams
With sweet water fays and dear little nixies
(Creations as fabulous as Florence Dixie's).
Mermaids sing by tars at the Isle of Vancouver
Untramelled by corset or new 'dress improver'
The moon shows their charms as on waves they are rocked
But if I describe them, perhaps you'd be shocked.
David Fitzgerald, Dublin.

July 16.
J. Webster, Glasgow.
I. Nennith, Glasgow.
July 17.
A. H. Mimmack, London.

Walter Daniell, London.
John Sugden Jnr, London.
John L Proud, London.

G. A. Seed, Sheffield.

James Monahan, Appleby, Westmorland.
July 18.
Walter F. Pemberton, Blackburn.
G. W. Pemberton, Lancaster.
The above named from Keswick via Sty Head Pass.

I with my daughter spent a very pleasant day or two at Mrs.
Tyson's. Had very nice weather, climbed under the kind guidance of
Mr. Bowring, the Great Gable and enjoyed the grand views. A
tolerable climb for a man in his 66th year.
D. Neve, Hurstpierpoint, Sussex.
*Before 1889 there was no right of burial in the churchyard at
Wasdale Head. It now contains the bodies of many climbers.*
July 19.
N. Illingworth Allison, Selby.
Charles Quinney, Selby.
Fred W. Davey, Leeds.

Frank Eastabrook, Clifton, Bristol.
July 20.
I. Bond, Liverpool.
James Hott,   do
En route for the Langdales via Boot.
*Chapel Stile is the village of Langdale. Holy Trinity Church here
was built in 1857 and has no windows on the north side.*
July 24.
John G. Jordan, Jarrow on Tyne.
From Buttermere by Scarf Gap and Black Sail Pass. To Keswick by
Sty Head Pass.
July 23.
Herbert Letts, London.
July 25.
Mrs. and Mr. White, Liverpool and Mr. and Mrs. Matthew,
London.
July 26.
James Spurr, Clare College, Cambridge.
July 28.
Mr. and Mrs. Sidney W. Bowser, Birkenhead.
Wm. Henry King, Liverpool and Dr. Syme, Egremont, Cumb.
*The ordinance of Richard Lucy for the government of the borough
of Egremont, made about the reign of King John, declared that those
who held burgage-tenure in Egremont were to find armed men for*

the defence of the castle, forty days at their own charge.

July 28.
Came from Buttermere by Scarf Gap and Black Sail Pass on a very hot day, and was hospitably received by Dame Tyson.
W. A. Webster, Sunderland.

The following was suggested to my mind after hearing that a man had visited this district and thought nothing of it:
No clouds rest on the mountain tops
O tis a glorious sight
From this deep vale to peer above
Mid heavenly calm and infinite love
To view them in the night.

Where is the heart that never felt
The bliss of solitude
Can there be one who e'er beguiled
While in this place 'neath mountain wild
His time in idle mood?

It cannot be that God's great works
Can scorned be by man,
Nay—let us all His works esteem
The works of He who doth redeem
Through Christ, that mighty plan.

W. A. Webster, Sunderland.   Sunday night July 29th.
July 30.
Jas. L. Thompson, Thomas D. Stockdale and Arthur Rainbank stayed at Dame Tyson's for luncheon. They were thoroughly satisfied with the hearty meal set before them.

R. Irons and Wm. Sharland, London.
From Rosthwaite to Buttermere July 30th and 31st. Were thoroughly satisfied with the accommodation provided.
July 31.
Jane Abbay and Eliza Stevenson, Rainton, Thirsk. Their third excursion from Seathwaite to Buttermere. Found Mrs. Tyson's a most comfortable house for ladies.
In the year 1769 Thomas Gray made his tour of the lakes. With his landlord from Keswick as a guide, Gray set out on the 28th October to explore the mountains in the vicinity of Seathwaite, in Borrowdale. He wrote that the scenery reminded him of the Alps.
August 1.
Clara E. F. Henley, Edinore Mills, Rye, Sussex.
Flo. R. Henley,   do   do
Maud C. Stonham, Rye, Sussex. ·
Edgar L. Stonham,   do   do
Walked from Dungeon Ghyll to WASTDALE via Sty Head Pass.

Lovely view. Magnificent day, nice walking, very good road.

R. P. Onions, Leeds.
Walked from Buttermere en route to Langdale and Coniston without smelling.

Mr. and Mrs. J. E. Horton, Liverpool.
Alfred and Robbie Horton, Liverpool.
Hope Rea, Eskdale.
Walter Rea, London.
The village of Coniston is at the western end of Coniston Water. The church of St Andrew was built in 1819. In the churchyard is the grave of John Ruskin, (1819-1900). Not far away is the Ruskin Museum.

August 2.
John Jones, Cottingham, Yorks.
R. Robinson,   do
J. W. Brown,   do
The usual firm....

William Talbot Bretherton, Runshaw Hall, Chorley.
Blanche Bretherton, sister to the above.
Alice Bretherton.
William Bretherton.
Elsie Bretherton.
August 3.
G. E. Grey, Tynemouth.

A. W. Bentham, London.
August 4.
George Herbert Brooke, Hanging Heaton, Dewsbury.
August 5.
E. Greenwood, Oxenhope, Keighley, Yorkshire.
Walter Greenwood, Hull, Yorkshire.
The third sea-port in the Kingdom.
August 6.
Robert Bennett Jnr, Buxton.
Clara Bennett, Westbourne, Buxton.

Rev. W. C. Bourne, Manchester.
Rev. Joseph Cooper, Egremont.

G. E. Moser, Kendal.
H. Moser, Kendal.
August 7.
W. Alfred Halliday.
Walked from Ambleside by Little Langdale, Rossett Gill and the Sty Head Pass. A fine day.

Green slate is plentiful around Elterwater in the Langdale Valley as shown by its extensive use in the surrounding buildings.

August 7.
Mr. and Mrs. F. W. Lockwood, Belfast.
Walked over from Boot on August 7th, a splendid day. August 8th it rained in torrents but had a splendid climb to Black Sail and view into Ennerdale. August 9th, started at 7.30 for Sca Fell Pike and on to Boot.

W. Thomas, Lancashire College, Manchester.
Wordsworth's poem 'The Brothers' was written after a visit in 1799 to the Old Chapel at Ennerdale Bridge. John Wordsworth, a relation of William, was the incumbent of the Old Chapel from 1824 to 1826.

August 8 to 15.
Thomas R. Bradshaw, M.D., B.A., Royal Infirmary, Liverpool.
August 6 to 11.
R. H. Everett, Canonbury, London.

J. G. Cheshire, Huntingdon Grammar School.
August 12.
J. Howlett, Darlington.
P. J. Cooper, Darlington.
John Forster, Durham.
F. Waddington, Leeds.
August 8 to 13.
J. G. Shotton, Curate of Wootton, Berkshire and wife.
August 15.
Fred E. Daniel, Harbourne, Birmingham.
Arthur J. Daniel.

W. R. England, Bingley.
T. H. Smith, Priesthorpe, Bingley.
August 16.
Walter Aston, London.
Allan Thomson, Bolton le Moors.
August 1 to 16.
George Hastwell, Darlington.
August 17.
Herbert Stanley Taylor of London, came here in great darkness and rain, and was clothed, warmed, fed, housed, and sent away in peace.

Once gain the mountain top and thou art free
Tis them who pause presume who turn to look are lost.
F. Wilson Fox, Rydal.
July 30 to August 18.
Barnard, Islington, London.

August 21.
Mrs. Thompson, Princess Park, Liverpool.
Miss Thompson.
August 22.
S. Woodward, London.

Rev. Sir F. L. Robinson, Cranford, Northants.
Lady Robinson.
August 22 and 23.
A. I. and T. Mitchell, London.
August 24.
Rev. E. B. Hicks, Alnwick, Northumberland.
William S. Hicks, Newcastle upon Tyne.
July 6 to August 24.
F. H. Bowring, London.
August 24.
J. E. Strange, Coleraine.
H. O'B. Newell, Dublin.
From Dungeon Ghyll, lovely day.

J. Morgan and Mrs. Morgan, Barrow in Furness.
Came over from Rosthwaite, a lovely day, a rough road over Sty
Head. Kindly received by Dame Tyson.
*Rosthwaite, in the Borrowdale valley, had all loads brought in on
horseback until the middle of the 18th century, when carts were used
for the first time.*

August 24 to 26.
N. Walls, Halliford, Middlesex.
August 25.
W. H. Williams, Southampton.

Robert Pratt, Barrow in Furness.

W. H. Bleakley, Birkenhead.
T. M. Bleakley,   do
From Derwentwater Hotel through Sty Head Pass returning through
Black Sail and Scarf Gap.
*The Tower Hotel, opposite the Derwentwater Hotel at Portinscale
near Keswick, was at the beginning of this century a college for
young gentlemen.*

August 28.
H. Masterman, Leyton, Essex.
Enjoyed it here very much, thanks to Mr. and Mrs. Tyson's
hospitality.

Jesse Herbert, Birmingham.
Hy. Glaisyer, Birmingham.

Miss Eva Clark.

Miss E. Lawson.

Miss E. Jorham.

Miss Lushington and party.

August 29.

Ernest W. Bennett.

August 30.

Mr. and Mrs. G. L. Barnard.

Visited cairn in Ennerdale and were very kindly received by Mrs. Tyson.

Arthur E. Priddin, Sunderland.

G. Harrison, Liverpool.

J. Wilkinson, Borrowdale.

August 31.

Very Good, 'T'.

September 1.

S. E. Higgins of Hampstead, London N.W.

R. W. Leach, London.

Arrived here on August 30th and were warmly received after a tiring walk from Dungeon Ghyll.

August 31st, ascended Scawfell in a dense fog but were more than repaid for the little exertion by the splendid views obtained during the descents.

Sept. 1st, leaving for Keswick via Black Sail, Scarff Gap and Buttermere, with some regret for leaving so kind a hostess.

A. H. Arkle, Claughton, Birkenhead.

D. D. Ireland.

September 3.

Miss Young spent three very pleasant weeks and has met with great kindness.

From Bedford.

September 4.

W. C. Beard, Nottingham.

Matt. W. Shelton,   do

Ada C. J. Wright, London.

Samuel Osborne Jnr, Sheffield.

William F. Osborne, Sheffield.

James A. B. B. Bruce, 2 Middle Temple Lane, London.

September 6.

Rev. T. Walker, Stratford, London, E.

Charles Davison, Sunderland.

John Clayton, Newburgh, Lancs.

September 5 to 7.

F. E. Atkinson, Whitefriars, Settle.

Mary Atkinson,   do

Alice Andrews, Cheltenham.

C. Terrey, Edinburgh.

September 9 and 10.
Rev. George Morris, St Stephens, Haggerston.
Rev. T. Nelson Burrow, St Augustine's Vicarage, Haggerston.

James B. Coulson, Derby.
September 12.
Rev. P. I. Richardson, St Phillip's, Dalston.

Frank Ackroyd, Bradford.
Kate Ackroyd.
May H. Ackroyd.
Lucy Ackroyd.
Annie Ackroyd.
J. E. A. and H. A. Ackroyd.
September 14.
A. J. Slade, Little Lever, Bolton.
C. J. Slade, Little Lever, Bolton, Lancs.

Laura Hayes, Ashley House, Handsworth, Birmingham.
William Hayes, 66 Gt. Russell Street, London.
W. P. and F. Turnbull, Stockwell End, Wolverhampton.
September 17.
A. D. Murray, Newcastle on Tyne.
Magnus Sandison,   do
September 18.
I. I. Carlyon, Emannuel College.
A. Hopkinson, Emannuel College.
The Mayor of Manchester.
Mrs Hopkinson.
Miss Browne, Heaton Mersey.
Miss Hopkinson, Manchester.
Miss N. Hopkinson, Manchester.
Miss G. Hopkinson,   do
Charles Hopkinson,   do
E. Hopkinson, London.
The Hopkinson brothers from Manchester were all enthusiastic climbers and, as the entry states, one was at this time Mayor of Manchester. In October 1887, a strong party led by the Hopkinson Brothers found a way down the outside face of Scafell Pinnacle to a point on the ridge within 100 feet of the first pitch in Deep Ghyll. There they built what is now known as Hopkinson's Cairn.

September 18.
I. W. B. MacLaren, Edinburgh.
- H. Waites, Darlington.
T. Banks, Darlington.

Swiss gentleman stayed all night and forgot to enter his name and left with the intention of ascending Scawfell Pikes.

Ernest E. Smallpage, Didsbury, Nr Manchester.

F. H. Edwards, 13 Croxteth Road, Liverpool.
H. Lupton, Roundhay, West Leeds.
September 22.
Mrs. Marsland Hopkins, Oxford.
Miss G. F. M. Hopkins, Holywell, Oxford.
Mrs. A. Commeline, Minster Yard, York.
Alice Commeline, Gloucester.
We arrived here without any rain. We have good hopes of another
fine day. Our second visit confirms the impressions of our first.
September 22 to 24.
R. Pendlebury, St Johns, Cambridge.
*R. Pendlebury was a regular visitor to Row Farm and became one of
the leading Lake District climbers. Later to become Professor
Pendlebury, he is remembered by the 'Pendlebury Traverse', a
variation of the ordinary route on the east face of Pillar Rock.*

September 27.
Mr and Mrs William Mann, St Leonards, Ashton upon Mersey,
Cheshire.
Remained with Mr. and Mrs. Tyson for a fortnight and duly
appreciated their kind hospitality.
October 2.
Lucy M. Pettitt, Keswick.
Bernard Thompson, Keswick.
October 21.
J. Heelin, Manchester.
L. Hulton,   do
L. Pilkington, do
H. Walker, Liverpool.
October 22.
George Nelson, Whitehaven. One night.
October 24.
Mr. and Mrs. Sibley, stayed with Mr. and Mrs. Tyson from
September 13th to October 24th.
Albert Villa, Saunders Street, Southport.
October 31.
Mrs. Wilson dined and slept in the same rooms in which her father
in law Professor Wilson (Christopher North) dined and slept 57
years ago.
Miss Wilson.
Miss M.A. Wilson, received a warm welcome from Dame Tyson.

*Professor Wilson was a giant of a man and heir to a large fortune.
As a very young man, he had fallen in love with Windermere and
bought a cottage at Elleray, later building a house there. Professor of
Moral Philosophy at Edinburgh University, he wrote articles in*

Blackwood's Magazine, under the nom de plume of 'Christopher North'. A great friend of Sir Walter Scott, Wilson also was in close contact with Wordsworth, De Quincey, Professor Sedgwick and the rest of that intellectual circle. Through his love of fell-running, wrestling and sailing, cock-fighting and fox-hunting, he came into contact with Will Ritson. An extrovert personality, with a great zest for life, Wilson was a happily married man, but still immensely popular with the ladies.

1884

June 24 and 25.
John W. Robinson, Whinfell Hall, Nr Cockermouth.
Mrs. Robinson,   do
Miss D. Harris, Derwent Bank, Broughton, near Carlisle.
Walked from Buttermere over Scarf Gap and Black Sail. Rain and mist on the latter. Were cordially received by Dame Tyson and well cared for. Intend to go over Scawfell Pikes to Keswick, on the 25th.
June 28.
J.H. Langley, Trinity College, Cambridge.
June 30.
Elliott Petre, Ellenborough.
Jno. E. McVitie,   do
Walked from Ellenborough (Maryport) via Loweswater, Crummock and Buttermere Lakes over Scarff Gap and Black Sail Passes to WASTDALE and were cordially received by Dame and Mr. Tyson.

Miss Newcombe,
Miss L.M.H. and B. Newcombe, Black Rock, Dublin.
A most comfortable lunch.
Edward Law, first Lord Ellenborough of Ellenborough, Maryport, was born in December 1750. Tradition says that he was born in the village of Ellenborough at a small cottage which has since been demolished, and on the site was built an infant's school. Edward Law was educated at St Peter's College, Cambridge, and then entered the Inner Temple as a law student. Having been called to the bar, he rose rapidly and was leading counsel in the defence of Warren Hastings. In 1801 Edward Law became Attorney General, and in 1802 was created Lord Ellenborough. Shortly afterwards, he was appointed Lord Chief Justice.

July 3.
Mr. and Mrs. N.E. Cant, Devonport.
From Rosthwaite, spent a day here and were very comfortable.
July 4.
L. Sutton, Redcar.
Stayed one night and departed highly gratified with my visit. Most hospitably treated in every possible way. Shall certainly repeat

my visit the first opportunity.

July 5.

A. Witney Marshall, Manchester.

J.P. Witney, Manchester.

July 6.

Percy Percival, Manchester.

From Whitehaven by Cleator Moor, Ennerdale and Windy Gap.

July 15.

Robert I. Fretwell, St George's Road, Hull.

A. Fretwell, 19 Rosamond Street, Hull.

Thomas Lister, Birkenshaw, Near Leeds.

William Lister, Gildersome, Leeds.

Jesse Clough, Shawfield, Tong, Nr Bradford.

Thomas Barker, Appleby.

July 14 and 15.

J.H. Kirkby, Queen's College, Oxford.

I.L. Hirst, Queen's College, Oxford.

July 19.

George F. Brown, Dearham, Maryport.

Richard Tyson Clark, Gosforth.

Mayson Penn, Gosforth.

The above visited Mosedale Waterfalls, WASDALE HEAD Church and were very kindly entertained by Dame Tyson on the aforesaid date.

Of the 600 people living in the parish of Gosforth, 115 died of the plague in 1657.

July 21.

E. Capper, Huyton, Liverpool.

Jessie Cooper,   do

Ada Cooper,   do

Percy Capper,   do

W.H.B. and Mrs. B. from Borrowdale, over Sty Head, now starting from Keswick via Black Sale and Scarff Gap, found a good appetite, which Mrs. Tyson has fully satisfied, as she did always.

A native of Borrowdale is sometimes called a 'Borrowdale Gowk', from the story of simple Borrowdale folk, who built a wall in an attempt to keep in the 'gowk' or cuckoo and so ensure perpetual spring.

July 21.

W. Ward Tamplin, Halifax, Yorks.

H.B. Johnson, Liverpool.

July 19 to 21.

J.A. Kempthorne, Trinity College, Cambridge.

July 22.

Mr. and Mrs. Scholefield, Dewsbury.

Bertie Scholefield.

Mark Napier Trollope, New College, Oxford.
Walter Hobshouse,   do
July 23.
Mattie G. Walker, The Brooklands, Leigh, Worcester.
Hannah E. Goodwin, Kidderminster.
Mary A. Goodwin, The Elms, Blakebrook, Kidderminster.
We came here wet, hungry and tired, but not sad. Dame Tyson
most kindly dried, clothed, fed and bedded us.
July 28.
Alfred Denny, Yorkshire College, Leeds.
Charles Edward Denny, Leeds.
Fred. W. Denny, Leeds (Third Visit).

J. P. C. Helton, Whitehaven.

Hugh Thomson, Elleray, London.

James H. Rea, Gatehouse, Eskdale.
July 30.
W.A. Kindley, Heaton Chapel, Stockport.
Alfred Blakemore, Bebbongton, Birkenhead.
July 31.
Harry Allen, Manchester.
Ernest McMichael,   do
Alfred McMichael,   do

Rev. W.E.C. Frith, Huntingdon.
C.A. Frith, Gainsborough.

Thomas Ashton, Manchester.
Albert Jordan, Manchester.
Keswick by Borrowdale and Honister Pass to Buttermere, then round
the lake and over Scarf Gap and Black Sail Pass on July 31st.
August 1.
W. Bealby, London.
A. Bealby,   do
From Ennerdale over Windy Gap (second visit).
Ennerdale Water is on the extreme edge of the western boundary of
the National Park; the nearest large town is Whitehaven.

August 3.
Tom Murray, Newcastle on Tyne.
A.D. Murray,   do
W. Harrison, Workington, Cumberland.
Joseph Howe, Workington, Cumberland.
Left Ennerdale via Windy Gap (in a thick mist) and arrived here at
10 o'clock. Very dark, on 3rd climbed Scawfell Pike via Piers Ghyll
and crawled up Strait Ghyll. Came down Mickledore and had tea,

and left for Buttermere by Black Sail Pass and Scarf Gap. Splendid view from top of Scawfell Pike. We were much indebted to Mr. and Mrs. Tyson for the very hospitable manner in which we were dealt with.

Workington had an old custom in the 19th century, when on Easter Mondays the men used to lift the women in the street by one leg and one arm. On Easter Tuesday the women did the same to the men.

August 3 and 4.
Herbert Mosen, Kendal.
Harry Robinson,   do
Alex   -   do
August 7.
P.W. Howard, Tottenham, London.
J.C. Howard, Poynton, Cheshire.
From Grasmere August 6th, ascended Scawfell Pike August 7th.
At Rydal, near Grasmere, there is a memorial window in St Mary's Church to William Fox, who died in 1887, and was Physician-in-Ordinary to Queen Victoria.

August 12.
George I. Wardle, Keighley, Yorkshire.
Andrew Smith,   do
H. Midgley, Keighley.
July 22 to August 12.
Reginald C. Broomfield, Trinity College, Oxford.
F.C. Clayton, Birmingham.
E.L. Squire, Coalbrookdale.
Harry   -
August 13.
Alfred Barnard, London.
Arthur H. Henderson, Highbury, London.
H. Roberson, St James, Gateshead.
J. Earl Norman, Stamford.
H.M. Ormesby, Rossall.
August 14.
T.H. Harper, Liverpool.
T.H. Peters,   do
Rev. H. L. Shillito, Blackburn.
Mrs Gibson, Hornsea, Hull.
Alec G. Gibson, aged 9.
G. McLean Gibson, aged 8.
A home from home.
The above six came over from Buttermere over Scarf Gap and Black Sail Passes and intend ascending Scawfell Pikes tomorrow.

Arthur Ransome, Bowdon.
L.H. Ransome.

M.E. Ransome.

E. Ransome.

A.C. Ransome.

Cockermouth, the nearest market town to the village of Buttermere, is built where the River Cocker joins the River Derwent, approximately on the site of a Roman settlement. Some of the town and also some of the castle is built of material taken from the ruins of the Roman fort. The Romans quarried the stone at Brigham and Broughton and the stones are marked with their wedge mark.

August 15.

The following party walked from Woodhouse, Buttermere to the Screes, Wastdale, and back; and on the return journey had an excellent tea at Dame Tysons:

Rev. P. Bowden Hinter, Rugby.

Mrs. E.P. Bowden Hinter.

Miss A. Bowden Hinter.

A. Bowden Hinter.

W. Bowden Hinter.

J.H. Bowden Hinter.

E.P. Bowden Hinter.

Miss Bowden Hinter.

Miss H. Bowden Hinter.

G. Bowden Hinter.

H. Bowden Hinter.

Examined and found correct...F.E. Kitchener.

Near to Wasdale Head is the village of Strands. A maypole was erected on the village green in 1897 to commemorate the Diamond Jubilee of Queen Victoria.

August 2 to 18.

This pleasant stay under Dame Tyson's hospitable roof was marked by rather more than the usual amount of climbing. Two ascents of the Pillar Rock were made; the first up by the East Route and down by the 'easy' way; the second up by the 'notch' and down by the West or Ennerdale Route. Both these ascents were undertaken by large parties. On the first occasion Mr. Michael Petty carried his guitar to the top of the Rock and entertained the company with songs. Nap and other games of cards were also played on the top of the Rock. On the second occasion Mr. Robinson of Whinfell Hall, W. Frith Bryden of London and Christopher Cookson of Corpus Christi College, Oxford, ascended the Rock straight up the Arrete over the notch, the first time this ascent has been made. Miss Bryden of Uffculme, Devon, who took part in both ascents, is probably the first lady who ever descended the Rock by the West Route. Miss Lucy Bryden and Miss Isobel Williamson ascended by the East Route and the notch respectively. Mickledore was also meanfully attacked from different sides. W. Frith Bryden and C. Cookson did the 'Penrith men's climb' from the right of Mickledore, and this route was afterwards followed by Mr. Robinson, Michael Petty, H.E. Cookson and Miss Bryden. The Chimney was also climbed by three exits. These expeditions were made under the experienced guidance of Mr. F.H. Bowring.

C.N. Williamson, St John's Wood, London.

August 14 to 15.
John W. Robinson, Whinfell Hall, Cockermouth, climbed with the above mentioned party, Pillar Rock, Penrith Men's climb and Mickledore and Chimney.

Charles Noel -Annfield.
Mrs. C. Noel - Annield.
C. Noel-Annfield.
Professor Turner and family, Edinburgh.
August 18.
Edward A. Scott.
Barbara Scott, both from Rugby.
From Buttermere returning same day.

Rev. P. Bowden Smith.
E.P. Bowden Smith.
G. Bowden Smith.
W. Bowden Smith.
From Buttermere via Great Gable, Great End, Scawfell Pike and Scawfell, down to Dame Tyson's and back to Buttermere in the evening.
Horse coaches would leave Keswick at 10 a.m. for Buttermere. They had a 30 minute stop at the Scafell and Royal Oak and at 11.30 they left for the journey over Honister Pass. At Seatoller, with the exception of the elderly, the remainder of the passengers left the coach and walked to the top. So terrifying was the descent into Buttermere, that many also walked down. A four horse coach carried 21 passengers and filled the 10 foot wide road. When at full gallop, with coach horns blowing and the coach brushing the hedge on both sides of the road, it was a spectacle which once seen was never forgotten.

August 18 to 19.
William Whiting, Headingley, Leeds.
A.M. Thorpe,   do
E.E. Thorpe,   do
August 17 to 19.
Edward L. Barnard, 137 Offord Road, London North.
Emily Barnard.
August 19.
J.J. Newell, London.
August 20.
Ernest Yeatherd, 4th Kings Own, Preston.

Herbert Stanely Tayler from Seascale.
'Et exiit nescius quo iret'. Drove here with a large party and up Scawfell with Miss Tayler on glorious day. See August 17th, 1883.
A.F. Tayler, Carlisle — from Seascale.

My dear Dame Tyson you must be a sinner
To make five starving fellows wait so long for their dinner
P.S. Mrs Tyson your'e a thorough nice 'un, and the dinner was worth the waiting.

T.E. Thomlinson, Carlisle.

R. Bott.
The church of St Cuthbert's, Seascale, has in the churchyard a memorial cross for the fallen of the 1914-18 war. Those who lost their lives in the 1939-45 war are remembered by the oak communion rail.

August 19 to 21.
Professor Arthur Cayley, Cambridge.
H. Cayley.
J.A. Thomlinson, Rossall.
H.F. Currie, Knothill, Carlisle.
P.R. Thomlinson, Englethwaite, Carlisle (Rossall).

August 14 to 22.
F.E. Kitchener, Schoolhouse, Newcastle, Staffs.
Mrs. F.E. Kitchener.
August 2 to 23.
Emma Williamson, London.
Isobel Williamson.
C.N. Williamson.
August 22 to 23.
T.H. Mason.
G. Mason, Rossall.

Agatha Richardson, Edinburgh.
Florence Swan,   do
Alicia Swan,   do
H.L. Richardson,   do
August 26.
Mr. and Mrs. Edward Keep, Melbourne, Australia.
Ronald Keep, Rugby School.
J.H. Baldwin, Halifax.
August 27 to 28.
W.B. Ferguson.
Bargrave Wilson.

A.A. Bowlby, London.
F.A. Bowlby.

W.W. Caroc, London.
I.F. Caroc.
Weather no better than this day two years ago, but Dame T. equally kind and hospitable. From Silverhow, Grasmere, via Esk Hause and Piers Ghyll.

Alfred A. Percival, London.
The ancient roads lay higher up the fell-side than those we use at the present time. For example, the road from Grasmere to Ambleside ran behind Rydal Mount along the side of Nab Scar. This is just another instance of how our ancestors avoided the valleys.

August 25 to 29.
Mr. and Mrs. F. Sheffield, Upper Norwood.
August 29 to 30.
Mr. and Mrs. C. Sankey, The Schoolhouse, Bury St Edmunds.
August 30.
F.L. Norris, Trinity College, Cambridge.
E.A. de Brett, Winchester College.
From Angler's Inn, Ennerdale.
The term 'Borrowin' Days' was used in the 19th century in the Ennerdale area. It denoted a fine day which came at an unexpected time—for example, a warm sunny day in March. The idea is that it is a day borrowed out of the summer months which will have to be paid back again.

August 31 to September 1.
John W. Robinson, Whinfell Hall, Lorton.
Pillar Rock, Gable and Chimney descended, the latter with W.P.H. Smith.
John W. Robinson, the legendary Cumbrian rock-climber, lived at Whinfell Hall, Lorton. Behind Lorton Hall is the famous yew-tree, beside which George Fox preached Quakerism when touring the district.

September 2.
J. Mather, Derby.
E. Nixon, Derby.
September 3.
Albert W. Skelton, Nottingham.
W.O. Beard, Nottingham.

G. James Wilson, Newcastle upon Tyne.
Thomas Jopling,   do

Leonard Courney and Mrs. Courney, Nelson.
September 5.
Rev. C. W. Hunt, Hartley Wintney, Hants.
P.L. Hunt, Brighton.

B.C. Hunt, Selwyn College, Cambridge.

Mrs. Robert Burbey, Clifton.
John L. Burbey, Clifton.
H.L. Smith, Clifton.
July 22 to September 5.
C. Cookson, Christ Church College, Oxford.
September 6.
Mrs Sargent, Rugby.
Miss Inglis, Beckenham.
Miss Julian Inglis, do
Mary Sargent, Sella Park.
Elinor D. Sargent,   do
G.G. Murray, St Johns College, Oxford.
E.B. Shekell, St Johns College, Oxford.
Near Sella Park, at Calderbridge, is Calder Abbey, founded in 1134 by the monks from Furness. It suffered at the hands of the Scots and was rebuilt many times.
September 8 to 10.
C. E. Hanson, Bradford, Yorkshire.
Emily Hanson,   do
Annie Eastwood, Bradford.
'Dry shoes and socks and borrowed bags they wore'.
September 6 to 8.
N. Walls, Halliford on Thames, Middlesex.
September 5 to 9.
I. R. Tanner, St Johns College, Cambridge.
Everett Leonoard Clifton, St Johns College, Cam.
August 30 to September 9.
H. McLeod Innes, Trinity Coll, Cambridge.
David Cowan, Trin. College, Cambridge.
July 18 to September 10.
F. H. Bowring, Hampstead, London.
September 11.
John Wood, 61 Wimpole Street, London.
Mrs. Wood and family.
Mrs. Mannder and the Misses Mannder.
J. E. Topham, 30 Gloucester Terrace, Hyde Park.

George Warrener, Darlington.
J. H. Waites,   do
J. W. S. Jennings, do
On our way from Ambleside we called at Kubleys, New Dungeon Ghyll Hotel, Langdale, faired moderately and found charges excessive. Dame Tyson serves us with excellent fare at moderate charge.
September 12.
Francis J. Chaplon, Fulbourn, Cambridge.

Howard F. Chaplin.
Gertrude M. Chaplin.
Annie K. Chaplin.

Miss A. Seeley, Windermere.
Miss E. L. Seeley, London.
Miss A. E. Seeley, London.

S. Ball, St Johns Coll, Oxford.
Edward Rathbone, Bassenfell, Keswick.
Published in 1855, a book on Windermere by Miss Martineau is most interesting. She tells us that the 'new buildings (and all are new) are of dark grey stone of the region, for the most part of a mediaeval style of architecture.'

September 12 to 15.
T. W. Bushill, Coventry.
F. Mitchell Smith, Coventry.
Coniston to Wastdale Head (or vice versa) via Walna Scar, Boot and Scafell. This is a very convenient route for those who want to see as much as possible in a short time, without overtaxing themselves. Though it is omitted from many guide books. Coming over Walna Scar (or the Old Man ad lib.) one descends on to the Duddon in the place recommended by Wordsworth and passes the scenes of his best sonnets. Lunch at the Travellers Rest in Ulpha, while same is preparing, a capital swim can be had in the Duddon, just below the Inn. On the way to Boot, inspect with care Stanley Ghyll. Stay the night at Tyson's Inn. The postmaster most obliging and will direct one to the 'diving pool' for the morning swim. Ascend from Boot, Scafell and Scafell Pike and come down into Wastdale by the Stye Head Tarn and Pass.
August 16 to September 15.
George Hastwell, Darlington.
September 10 to 15.
H. Bertram Cox, Christ Church College, Oxford.
H. Y. Oldham, Jesus College, Oxford.
September 15.
S. G. Sheppard, Herts.
E. B. Sheppard.

Long shall I remember.
The 15th of September.
When lived a jaded I and Ted
Tramped across the rough Sty Head
Good Dame Tyson's fare that we might test
Knowing there that we should get nothing but the best.
I shall neer forget, what's more,
The snug old bed in number four.
There I slept a good twelve hours

Got up in time to see that showers
Were so fast descending, that we guessed
Our view from Scawfell Pike would be anything but the best.
Sure I mustn't now forget
Ere out upon my bridge I set
To tell you not to keep aloof
From this good couple's cheery roof
But when the chance affords, this house pray test
For you cannot grumble where you get all that you request.

September 18.
- Rutley, London.

Frederick Littleboy, Sunderland.

Mrs. Prout Newcombe, Croydon, Surrey.
Bertisa Newcome,   do
Mabel Newcombe.
Jessis W. Newcombe.

September 21.
Yesterday in company with Mr. W.P. Haskett-Smith climbed from the 'Lord's Rake' end of the 'Rake's Progress' straight up to the top of the 'Pinnacle Rock' of Scawfell, being the second recorded ascent of this Rock, the first ascent was made by W. P. H. S., Esq, some weeks ago by the short 'slab' route near the top by which way we descended. You enter our climb of yesterday about 60 yards from the (? North) end of the 'Rake's Progress', a slight detour to the right hand lands you at the foot of a steep, narrow gorge, up which no difficulty is experienced to a height of about 300 feet, you are then faced by a 150 feet of almost perpendicular chimney in which the holds are small, but sound as far as they go. Arriving at a point, where the chimney is lined with rotten moss, a few careful steps to the right bring you out onto a broad ledge, pass along about 20 yards onto the aréte, which leads up to the 'Pinnacle' Rock above.
A short scramble from this point lands you on the lower summit of the Pinnacle Ridge from which you look down a perpendicular wall into 'Deep Ghyll'. Here we built a good sized cairn of stones. Nothing now remains but a scramble up the very steep aréte to the top, where you observe a cairn built by W.P. Haskett-Smith on his first ascent from what may be called the Pisgah Rock and Pisgah Gap Side, a few weeks ago. This name is rather a good one, as the resemblance to the Pillar Rock 'Pisgah' is striking. The climb up the latter part of the aréte is charming, as the holds are splendid in comparison to the previous experience in the chimney below. On the top you will observe in a hole in the cairn a bottle, in which to deposit visiting cards. To descend from here into the Pisgah Gap there is no great difficulty, as the holds, if not numerous, are sound.
—J. W. Robinson, Whinfell Hall, Cockermouth.

September 19 to 21.
Frederick W. Jackson, Bolton.
Witnessed the above climb, but it can only be done by the boldest climbers.

John Wilson Robinson, of Whinfell Hall, Lorton, near Cockermouth, was a regular visitor to the Tysons. Born in 1853 into a Quaker family, he was educated at Friends School, Ackworth. His death took place in 1907 at Brigham where he was buried. In at the beginning of climbing in the Lake District, he did most of his climbing with Walter Parry Haskett-Smith, and it is worth recording that he described this Cumbrian as well built, bald, with sandy whiskers and merry blue eyes. Robinson also climbed in the Himalayas with that great mountaineer J. Norman Collie. He was with Collie on the first ascent of Moss Gill when the famed 'Collie Step' was cut.

John Robinson and George Seatree, the latter a corn dealer from Penrith and a native of Alston, spent a week in 1885 camping below Pillar Rock and then in Upper Eskdale. It is generally believed that these two were the first people to combine camping and climbing in Lakeland. On this occasion a proper climbing rope was used for the first time in the Cumbrian mountains. Following their week under canvas, Robinson and Seatree availed themselves of the home comforts with Mrs. Tyson at Row Farm for the last four days of their holiday.

Robinson kept a diary and recorded his mountain walks and climbs. First entry is the ascent of Scafell Pike on June 23rd, 1874, when he was about 22 years old. He climbed Pillar Rock (his favourite) 101 times; Scafell Pinnacle over 50 times; made nearly 40 ascents of Great Gable; Helvellyn five times and Skiddaw only on four occasions. In all he recorded 348 rock and mountain climbs. The first time he climbed Pillar Rock was in 1882.

The High Level Route to Pillar was his discovery, and it is appropriate his memorial, the 'Robinson Cairn', should stand at one end of this traverse within a stone's throw of this great rock upon which he helped to make history. It overlooks the Ennerdale he knew and loved so well and faces across the fells to his ancestral home. The 'Robinson Cairn' was built by his friends under the direction of Haskett-Smith in his memory on Easter Saturday 1908. The same year a tablet was fixed on to a face of rock near to the cairn. The inscription reads, 'For Remembrance of J. W. R. of W. H. in Lorton.'

John W. Robinson was also a great walker and on one occasion he walked over the principal summits of the lakes, a total of 70 miles, in 24 hours. This genial dalesman, a celebrity in his life-time, is remembered as a great climber, great wit, story-teller and a man with a great love of his native fells.

September 20 to 21.
Mr. and Mrs. Cunine, Birkenhead.

October 2.
Mr. and Mrs. Plaque and Miss Beatrice Potter, Gloucestershire and London.

Alex Munro, Lancaster.
October 5.
I. K. F. Cleabe, Hertford College, Oxford.
October 6 to 8.
John S. Mawson, Keswick.
Stanley Pearson, Manchester.
October 11.
William Wills, Inner Temple, London. E.C.
James Frederick Burton, Lincolns Inn Fields, London.
December 24 to 30.
R. L. Harrison, London.
Claude Wilson, Edinburgh.
H. Wilson, Cambridge.
Francis E. Wilson, Macclesfield.
Much snow, in good order — excellent. Rocks mostly glazed. Beautiful weather.
December 27 to 31.
H. Woolley, Manchester.

1885-1886

January 12.
W. Nile, Boston, Lincs.
B. W. Staniland,   do
February 13.
Cecil Spring Rice.
Gerald Spring Rice.
February 28 to March 2.
William Cecil Slingsby, Carleton, Skipton.
John Arthur Slingsby,   do
William Ecroyd, Nelson in Marsden.
Geoffrey Hastings, Bradford.
Cuthbert Hastings, Silsden.
Spent three days amongst the peaks with ice axes and ropes and found the snow in most splendid order, were five hours climbing gullies and couloris about the Pillar Rock.
Among the many famous rock-climbers who were regular visitors to Row Farm was William Cecil Slingsby, a Yorkshire dalesman. Born in 1849, he was a member of a wealthy family living at Carleton, Skipton. Educated at Cheltenham School, he first climbed in Norway and the Alps with Geoffrey Hastings. These two gentlemen paid their initial visit to Row Farm in 1885. An all-round mountaineer, W. C. Slingsby was stalwart, broad-shouldered, full bearded, with a classic profile, and laughing grey-blue eyes, full of vitality. A plaque to his memory was unveiled by John Wilson Robinson of Whinfell Hall on Pillar Rock.

March 3 to 4.
Henry R. Procter, Tynemouth.
John W. Robinson, Whinfell Hall, Lorton.
March 21 to April 17.
C. Cannan, Trinity College, Oxford.
H. E. D. Blakiston, Trinity College, Oxford.
A. T. Quiller Couch, Trinity College, Oxford.
Arthur Quiller Couch, a teacher of English Literature at both senior universities in turn, also wrote under the pseudonym 'Q' and spent three Easter vacations at Row Farm, climbing and writing. A

*connoisseur of good food, in an article he described a Mrs. Tyson
speciality, named by her 'Pendlebury Pudding' after one of her rock-
climbing guests. The dish was a delicious compound of farm milk,
tapioca and raisins.*

March 21 to 27.
A. R. Atkinson, Christ College, Oxford.
March 29 to April 7.
Rev. H. G. Woods, Trinity College, Oxford.
April 2 to 11.
W. Little, Christ College, Oxford and Lincolns Inn.
A. L. Mumm, Christ Church College, Oxford and Inner Temple.
A. F. Peterson, Christ Church College, Oxford and Inner Temple.
April 7.
F. G. Luard, Wadworth Vicarage, Doncaster.
H. C. Armour, Rossall.
April 2 to 10.
J. Clay, St Johns College, Cambridge.
C. F. Clay, Trinity College, Cambridge.
April 3 to 10.
M. C. Potter, Peterhouse, Cambridge.
April 7 to 15.
H. McLeod-Innes, Trinity Coll. Cambridge.
J. A. Kempthorne, Trinity College, Cambridge.
April 12 to 15.
R. C. Gibson, Trinity College, Cambridge.
J. H. Knowles, Trinity College, Cambridge.
J. P. Gibson, Haileybury.
April 16 to 20.
T. G. Creak, Emmanuel College, Cambridge.
S. O. Roberts, Joh, Cambridge.
April 23.
V. S. Jones, Burneside, Kendal.
H. G. Jones, Haileybury.
Alice M. Jones, Burneside, Kendal.
Agnes H. Jones   do
Ethel M. Crewdson, St Georges Vicarage, Kendal.
S. M. Crewdson,   do
April 24.
Rev. Canon Trotter, Vicarage, Alnwick.
April 16 to 29.
C. H. Hodgson, St Margarets Vicarage, Altrincham.
W. B. Wildman, Westbury, Sherborne, Dorset.
H. R. King, Sherborne School.
J. Moore,   do

Louisa Shaw, Harrogate.
Emily Pickard, Hawkshead.

Florence Randall, Bridport, Dorset.
May 5 to 7.
D. W. Samways, St Johns College, Cambridge.
H. Arnold Bourne, Clare College, Cambridge.
May 7.
J. C. Read, Newcastle upon Tyne.
L. Johnston,   do
May 24.
S. H. Farr, Kennington Road, London.
R. D. Mounsey, London.
Mrs. Tyson's is much better than the Inn.

Miss Bailey, Frizing Hall, Bradford.
Miss C. E. Bailey,   do
Mr. F. A. Bailey.
May 24 to 26.
P. H. Lockwood, Kendal.
Photographed 'Deep Ghyll Pillar' — from first limb of Lord's Rake
right hand wall in ascending, also from a ledge jutting out into
opposite side of Deep Ghyll.

Arnold H. Robson, Sunderland.
Walter Sherwell Jordan, Sunderland.
Crossed from Scafell Pikes to Scafell by Broad Stand which was
highly dirty and slippery from melting snow, patches of which
obscured the route upwards from Broad Stand.

John Redhead, Barrow in Furness.
Eli Beckett,   do

The sun was sinking in the far, far, west,
When Redhead and Beckett retired here to rest;
In leaving here they were much distressed,
Though starting to mount Great Gable's breast.

Accommodation good—i' faitte!
Saithe the undersigned
H. Snaithe,
Arrived from Lincolnshire and Boston
- a coast where ships are often lost on -
In May, year 1885
Oh! years may kind Dame Tyson thrive.

May 27.
Mrs. H. Snaith.
May 28.
A bright bit for wanderers in Wastdale
Remember the Sun is always shining - somewhere.
Always look for the sunny side

149

And if life troubled be
With a prayer-full heart bid care depart
And God will comfort thee.
Charles Westall Marsden, Blackburn.
Benjamin W. Marsden.

I. N. Watson, Blackburn.
May 16 to 30.
Mrs. and Miss Strong, Glasgow.
Beside the Gosforth and Holmrook road in the Wasdale area, there was a cottage known as Mary Larg's, which was used by smugglers to hide their goods. Mary is reputed to have been convicted of smuggling and hung on the local gallows hill. The place where the cottage stood is now known as Marylands.

May 28.
The following poem by A. H. Geyer appears in the Visitor's Book in German and has been translated into English in the book by F. H. B.:
FAREWELL TO WASTDALE
The Mountains are my native home,
The Mountains — loved where'er I roam,
Where-ever I may find them:
O'er glaciers in my Alpine land,
If on Ben Nevis' brow I stand,
Or climb Sca-Fell Pikes summit.

The Mountains all to me are dear,
God's gift to me His Creature here,
A token of His favour;
When I descry them I am gay,
And sad when I must wend my way,
Back to the cities' hubbub.

And Mountains here too I have found,
In Wastdale's mountain hold of ground,
And then I have ascended;
And now we must at last depart,
I bear your image in my heart,
Ye well-beloved Mountains.
— A. H. Geyer, Linz, Austria.

May 29.
J. Entwisle, Deane, Nr Bolton.
May 29 to June 1.
H. R. Cottrill, 58 Denmark Road, Manchester.
June 1.:
A. E. D. White, London.
Herbert Gray, London.

June 3.
Agnes Smith, Holmwood, Weston Super Mare.
Mary Smith.
Eleanor Smith.
June 6.
Henry Brown Junior, Highfield, Luton.
Edward Brown,   do
June 9.
J. T. Ware, York.

Rev. M. R. Allnutt, and Mrs. Allnutt, AllHallows, Leeds.
Very comfortable accommodation for the night.
June 11 to 15.
A. E. Peile, Workington.
June 12 to 15.
George Seatsee, Penrith, and Mr. J. W. Robinson.
Spent the night of the 11th camping out in Great Doupy Pillar at
an elevation of 2,100 feet. Had a fine time of it—climbed together
up 'Right hand Pisgah'. J. W. R. also ascended by 'Corner' direct
from slab, it is supposed that Dr. Whitehead ascended this way in
1850.
*George Seatree, a corn dealer of Penrith, created history when with
John Wilson Robinson he camped at the foot of Pillar, the two being
the first to camp and climb with the use of a rope. Seatree discovered
the North Climb in 1874, when climbing the Scafell cliffs from
Mickledore.*

June 15.
A. Scott, Newcastle upon Tyne.
G. O. Owen Jnr (distinguished), Newcastle upon Tyne.
June 16.
C. E. Pearson, Notts.
J. D. Pearson,   do
H. Orton,   do
From Thirlmere to Lodore.
*At the head of Thirlmere lies Wythburn with its small church. This
was a favourite meeting place for picnics with the Wordsworth and
Coleridge families when the Wordsworths lived in Grasmere and the
Coleridges at Keswick.*

June 18.
H. G. Weeks, Bromley, Kent.
June 18 to 20.
Rev. J. S. Charlton, St Marys, Barnsley.
Miss Charlton, Northallerton.

R. Tyson, Beacon Hill, Penrith.
June 23 to 24.
Wm. Bell, Liscard, Cheshire.

June 8 to 25.
F.H. Bowring, Hampstead, London.
By Aneroid, Height of Row Head 274·5 feet; Mickledore (Lowest Point) 2746; Pillar of Deep Ghyll and Pinnacle Rock, Scawfell 3145 feet; D. of Lingmell 2600 (nearly).

Howard S. Bliss, New York City, USA.
June 25.
Robert Grierson, Hexham on Tyne.
E. Turnbull,　　　do
June 26.
John P. Mulcaster, Benwell, Northumberland.
June 27.
Mrs. and A. P. Allan walked from Keswick, splendid day, very hot, and on to Coniston on Monday. From Penge, London.
June 30.
John Bolton, London.
John W. Bolton, London.
Robert C. Bolton, London.
July 3.
Miss Burzacott, Brisbane, Queensland, Australia.
Miss A. Burzacott,　　　do
W. J. Burzacott,　　　do
Very much pleased with the attention paid them after struggling from Buttermere over Scarff Gap and Black Sail.
June 29 to July 4.
Elizabeth and Sarah Jane Tyson came from Beacon Hill, Penrith, via Carnforth and Drigg on June 29th and stayed here until July 4th, and spent a most delightful week with their kind and hospitable cousins, had most beautiful summer weather all the time and thoroughly enjoyed the lovely scenery, the pure air, the rest and quiet of this most peaceful dale.
July 9.
James McMullen, Blackburn.
A. M. Wandless, Parton, Whitehaven.

Mr. and Mrs. Robert Ellis, Exeter.

Mr. Walter Kenyon, Oldham.
Mr. James Storey, Oldham.
July 13.
Octavius and Nonus Smith came from Keswick by coach to Buttermere, thence through Scarff Gap and Black Sail Pass. Found everything here very comfortable, etc. Much credit due to Dame Tyson.
Canon Harford-Battersby, vicar of St Johns, Keswick, organised the first Keswick Convention in 1875. He was assisted by Robert Wilson, of Broughton Grange near Cockermouth, who was a Quaker. That first Convention was attended by some 400 people. Today it has a world-wide reputation.

152

July 17.
Edward Parkinson, Rochdale.
John Henry Crabtree, Rochdale.
July 19.
David B. Monsoa, 28th Bo. N. I.
July 20.
George Butterfield, Sunderland.
Michael Robson, Sunderland.
S. Burnham, Manchester.
M. Rodgers, Manchester.
T. P. Davies, Darwen.
W. H. Ewald, St Johns Vicarage, Lancaster.
Walked from Boot, found Tyson the guide pleasant and civil.
In Boot in the Eskdale area it was customary on Christmas Day to eat a giblet pie, to which were added black puddings made of goose's or pig's blood mixed with unrendered lard finely shredded, shelled oats, and seasoned with cornmint.

July 22.
Isabella Horne, Waterford.
Thomas B. Horne, Brighton.
Walked from Gatesgarth over Black Sail.
The ancient system of marking sheep for identification purposes is still in use. Gate's Shepherd's Guide for Cumberland published in 1879 has the following entry:- 'Edward Nelson: Gatesgarth, Buttermere; Fleetwith Stock, under key-butted near, two strokes over couplings, wethers black on head, twinters red.'

July 23.
Fred Marples, Duffield, Derbyshire.
From Keswick to Buttermere up to Scale Force over Scarff Gap and Black Sail to Mrs. Tyson's.
Oh ye Gods what a path.

William Bell, Melbourne, Derbyshire.

H. S. Child, London.
The real invasion of the lakes by tourists commenced in the 19th century, principally through the writings of the Lake Poets. Wordsworth in 1799 was living at Grasmere. In 1800 Coleridge was at Keswick, where he was joined in 1803 by Southey. De Quincey in 1834 published his 'Reminiscences of the Lake Poets', in which he described the daily lives of his neighbours, Wordsworth, Coleridge and Southey.

July 24.
I climbed the dark Brow of the Mighty Helvellyn
I hope you don't doubt it's the truth that I'm telling

The same day I went up the gloomy Scawfell
Yet somehow or other I don't feel quite well
I rode round the lake here without more ado
I hope you don't doubt what I'm saying is true
And walked round Windermere on to Keswick
Yet somehow or other I feel very ----
— George Pearce, Edgbaston.
*Budworth, writing in 'A Fortnight's Ramble to the Lakes', published
in 1792, is one of the few Lakes' writers in the 18th century who
was interested in fell-walking. He climbed Helvellyn, Skiddaw,
Coniston Old Man and the Langdale Pikes.*

July 22 to 24.
The man who here lodges is surely a wise'un
And won't repent visiting good Dame Tyson;
For I venture to say, without being oracular,
That her house (though externally far from spectacular)
Is in comfort and cleanliness hard to excell
Though you searched all the land you could see from Scafell.
— A. E. Molyneux, London.

Frederick W. Payne, London.
Eustace A. Payne, London.
July 23 to 24.
E. J. ---- Blackheath, Kent.
James A. Neell, Greenwich, Kent.
Arrived here weary and footsore after a long day's walk from Lodore
via Buttermere, Scale Force, Scarff Gap and Black Sail (nearly
26 miles). Roads over Honister and the two latter passes very
unpleasant. Now bound for Coniston.
July 25.
Lily Beaumont, Cheetham Hill, Manchester.
Fanny G. Beaumont, Southport.
Mr. and Mrs. G. Beaumont, Cheetham Hill, Manchester.

H. B. Spencer, The Styes, Sowerby, Yorkshire.
Mrs. Spencer,   do

Fanny Marie Beaumont, Manchester.
Thomas and Mrs. Middleton, Didsbury.
July 27.
Ryan Martin, Tunbridge Wells.

James H. Lansdell, Hastings.

John Curran, Felling, Newcastle upon Tyne, arrived here at 4.p.m.,
from Rosthwaite after an exhausting walk over Sty Head. To
Keswick tomorrow (for a new pair of shoes, one pair having

succumbed to the rocks and stony road of Sty Head and The Rake).
Work again on Thursday alas.

Bassenthwaite village near Keswick is dominated by Skiddaw, which at 3,054 feet is the fourth highest mountain in England. The earliest recorded ascent of Skiddaw was by Bishop Nicholson in 1684. The village has two churches — St Bega's founded in 640AD and St Johns in 1878.

July 28.
Benjamin West, Belgrave, Leicester.
R. Guy Waddington, Leicester.
July 29.
Mr. and Mrs. A. W. George, Sydenham.

Allan Jesper, Scar Bank, Levens, Westmorland.
Walter Jesper.
Edward W. Jesper.

Thomas Hoole, Battersea, London.

A. James Flann, Heaton, Newcastle upon Tyne.
John F. Richardson, Byker, Newcastle upon Tyne.
July 30.
J. Severn Bateson, Greenside, Kendal.
Joseph H. Bateson,   do

George O. Foy, Leeds, Yorkshire.
Bedford Foy, New College, Oxford (Leeds).
August 3.
Claude Shoolbred, London.
August 1 to 3.
R. Ainslie, Sedbergh School.
August 3.
Jonathan Moore, Chester le Street, Durham.
Thomas Moore, Eastgate.
August 4.
W. F. Pemberton, Blackburn.
Nathan Neville, Blackburn.
George William Pemberton, Blackburn.

R. Bowring, Ullswater Hotel.
August 6.
Herbert and Henry Mackie, Leeds.
August 5 to 6.
Rev. William Ward, Hadleigh, Suffolk.
A. G. Ward, St Pauls School, London.
August 6.
Albert Carless, MRCS, Richmond, Surrey.

J. H. Greene, Kew, Surrey.
Found this house a very pleasant rest, there is no better rest in Christ. Matt XI 28.

Arthur Edward Sharpley, Handsworth, Staffs.

E. Blair Allen, Tow Law, Darlington.

John Bond, Liverpool.
W. J. Sutherland, Liverpool.
Thomas Holt, Jnr, Liverpool.
James Holt, Liverpool.
The above party of four have been wandering about the hills and dales of Cumberland for the last week, under the blind and reckless guidance of the first named, infatuated individual—J. Bond.
Stephenson's Guide Book was 'The light to our feet and lamp to our path', but its illuminating influence was considerably clouded by the obscure intellect of the above anathemalistic guide and the mischievous propensities of the member of our party named Thomas Holt.

August 8.
Miss Spence, North Shields.
Miss Corder, Sunderland.
J. W. Corder, Sunderland.
Walter Corder, Sunderland.
J. W. Robinson, Whinfell Hall, Cockermouth.
James Watson, North Shields.
Eaglesfield near Cockermouth is a village which has a claim to fame in the history books. Robert Eaglesfield, a native of the village, was confessor to Edward III's Queen and was also the founder of Queen's College, Oxford, where he was buried in 1349. Fletcher Christian was born at nearby Moorland Close in 1764 and is remembered for his part in the 'Mutiny on the Bounty' and the founding of the colony at Pitcairn Island. John Dalton, born here in 1766, was the first developer of the atomic theory. At the age of 12 he taught in the village school and died in Manchester in 1844.

August 8.
Henry Byke.
Walter Byke.
Jolly wet, rough and windy from Seathwaite to Wastwater.

R. J. Girling, Ipswich.
Thought there was a great wast of water here. It rained one day and poured the next.

George Lowe, 106 Wilmslow Road, Rusholme, Manchester.
Agrees with the above sentiments.

August 12.
H. C. Jackson, Merton, Melbourne, Australia.

G. Mc. C. Campbell, Rodwell Cottage, ----------

Rev. C. R. Gilbert, Clifton Green House, York.
August 13.
Mr. and Mrs. Wood, Manchester.
Mr. and Mrs. Wharton, Birkenhead.
With their respective families, in all eight persons drove from
Seascale, lunched very comfortably at Mrs. Tyson's.

H. Pilcher and two sons of Manchester. From Drigg.

E. H. Batchelor, Leeds.
W. W. MacPherson, Leeds.
Rev. J. F. Longrigg, Shipley.
August 14.
A. Strand, Hinckley, Leicestershire.

H. W. Sillifant, London.

R. H. S. Cooper, Dublin.
Miss C. Cooper.
Miss M. Cooper.
John Gilmour.

A down a flowing beck we came
I really cannot tell the name
It matters not but where it flowed
Most deeply as it crossed the road.
Some-how my right foot chanced to slip
Which gave me an unpleasant dip
I sank, but quickly rose again
And here I must my pen refrain
From telling what my lips let fall
Of sharp reproach against them all
For letting me fall in. I rose
And struggled on to find repose
A downy bed, dry shoes and dress
Which weary travellers in distress
Will find that the kind hosts supply
To those, who on their faith rely.

H. Biedeman, Batavia.
Gustave Hoche, Paris.
August 15.
Ninetta Lambertini, Hyde Park, London.

Emma Lambertini,   do
Fanny Merricks, Kensington, London West.

Mr. Mrs. and Miss Cooper, and Mr. Tom Cooper.
Mr., Mrs. and the Misses Clapham.
Mr. and Mrs. Le Jeune, all of Manchester.
August 18.
Carl P. Frin-
Climb ------Ambleside.

Fred Pickard, 12 Harold Street, Sunderland.
Snowdon Chapman, 2 Amberley Street, Sunderland.

Rev. Walter D. May, Durham.
Miss C. E. May, Painswick, Stroud.
August 19.
Thomas Thomson, Witherington, Manchester.
Alfred Hy Terry,   do

Guided by the light in a window of the hospital farm, we weary travellers found rest at 10.15 p.m., after walking from Thirlmere by way of Watendlath, Lodore and Seathwaite and the Stye Pass. Ye travellers who would see Stye Head, go traverse it in the pale moonlight as we did.
Florence Balgarnie, Scarborough.
---Ashley, Scarborough.

John Haigh, Keighley.
J. W. Graham, London.
T. J. Wallas, London.
Chapel Sunday was formerly celebrated in the Watendlath area. This was a Sunday set apart annually in August, when people assembled from a distance and heard divine service. They afterwards dined with their friends and then adjourned to the inns to make merry in honour of the saint to whom the chapel (church) was dedicated.

August 20.
Wm. John Sowerby, Darlington.
John Alex Fothergill, Darlington.
Walter Brunskill, Darlington.
Went up Pillar Rock by 'ledge', came down by 'notch'. Scrambled in the afternoon as far as convenient up Piers Ghyll and afterwards to the Greta Falls. Time from Mrs. Tyson's to the top of Pillar, 2 hours and 5 minutes.
August 21.
W. H. Hillier, London. S.E.
Exceedingly comfortable. A home from home.

Rev. Bowden Smith.
Miss A.
Miss H.
G. B. S., Ball Coll.
W. B. S., Rugby.
H. B. S., Rugby.
J. R. B. S., Rugby.
Walked over from Buttermere down to Wastwater and back to
Buttermere. Excellent tea as usual.

Rowland Baxter, Cleator Moor.
Thomas Golightly, Cleator Moor.
From Eskdale.
*The most direct route to Wastwater from the southern part of the
county is over the long and difficult passes of Wrynose and Hard
Knott. These lead into the Eskdale Valley. The road route to
Wasdale runs down the valley to Eskdale Green, on to Santon
Bridge, then north-east to Wasdale. The walker's route goes up the
Whillan Beck, past Burn Moor Tarn down into Wasdale Head.*

August 21.
Charles Wm. Hooper, Whitehaven.

Rev. H. Richmond Deck, Hull.
Rev. Ernest Barry, Beverley.

John C. Luch, Whitehaven.

Mr. and Mrs. Watson, Spital, Cheshire.
Mrs. Moodie, Rock Ferry, Cheshire.
Wm. Catterall, Preston.
Could not have been more comfortable.
August 24.
E. W. W. Carlier, Norwich.
P. Lawson, Hull.
W. Lawson, Hull.
August 25.
Maurice D. Blunt.
E. Blunt.

Mr. and Miss Pritchard, Mr. Walls and Mr. Ware started from
Wasdale Head, went up Great Gable by Sty Head, thence up Scafell
Pike by Esk House and on to Mickledore descending Lingmell.
Pritchard and Walls went part of the way up the 'Chimney' and
then up the first stretch of the Lord's Rake, which latter they found,
as the truthful Jenkinson says, 'laborious climbing'. The days work on
the part of the lady was very good and deserved recording, to the
'general' and the 'gentle shepherd'.

Irton Hall in the Wasdale area has a ghost. It was last seen over 100 years ago. A lady in black with white lace is said to come out of a cupboard in the corner of the tower room and go to the window to gaze out. It may be the ghost of Margaret Broughton, the daughter of a Yorkist house and the wife of the man who refused the king shelter. The curious part of the story is that the cupboard in question, which always figures prominently, marks an obliterated and long forgotten entrance which must have opened on to the original newel stair of the tower.

August 23 to 25.
N. Walls (The General).
August 17 to 27.
J. T. Ware, 6 New Street, York.
Found the place very comfortable and received every attention from Mr. and Mrs. Tyson.
August 22 to 27.
Miss Pritchard, Croydon.
E. Pritchard, C.C.C., Camb.
H. J. Enner, London.
H. Bassett, London.
August 27.
Mr. and Mrs. Plant, Preston.
J. C. Baker, Eccles.
Philip Burtt, York.
Geo. Burtt, York.
S. H. Wright, Mansfield.

W. F. Langbehn, Newcastle on Tyne.
J. H. Langbehn, Newcastle on Tyne.
August 28.
J. E. Smith, Bury, Lancs.
Then flashing back one lingering glance on River, Lake and Fell
We quit the bright scene murmuring regretfully farewell.

J. Stock, Bury, Lancs.

Jackson Bennett, Bradford.
Arthur McBarnie, Bradford.

Mrs. Samuel Burgess, Oldham.
John W. Burgess, Oldham.

Gerald Peck, Southport.
Ernest W. Hardman, Manchester.
August 30.
Mr. C. Heald, Wisbech.
Edward J. Robson, Darlington.

J. Bennett Gibbs, Darlington.
E. A. Brayshaw, Guide.
August 31.
Ambrose Blakey, Peterborough.
August 30 to 31.
Rev. R. F. Cobbold, The School House, Macclesfield.
P. A. Cobbold, Colchester.
September 2.
Wm. Raine Selwood, High Street, Wandsworth.
James Woolley, Dorking, Surrey.
September 3.
-A. Overton, Exeter College, Oxford.
G. Broderick, Haileybury.
K. W. Broderick,   do
We arrived very wet and miserable after a stormy walk from
Buttermere over Scarf Gap, Black Sail and were most hospitably
received by Mr. and Mrs. Tyson.
September 4.
Ed. Brunskill, Penrith.
Tom A-, Penrith.

September 8.
Mrs. Sargent, Rugby.
Miss Sargent, Sella Park.
Miss K. Sargent, Sella Park.
Miss G. D. Sargent,   do
Miss Marion Sargent, Rugby.
J. H. Sargent, Exeter College.
W. D. Sargent, Merton College.
Miss Evelyn Wybergh, Overton Hall.
Wilfred J. Wybergh, Winchester Coll.
Miss Inglis Binfield, Beckenham.
Miss J. M. Inglis,   do
Miss Bowden Smith, Rugby.
Miss Alice Bowden Smith, Rugby.
Miss Helen Bowden Smith,   do
Miss Nonement, Waborne.
Mr. Arthur Bowden Smith.
Mr. F. H. Bowden Smith, Trin. College, Oxford.
Mr. G. Bowden Smith, Ball Coll.
Mr. W. Bowden Smith, Rugby School.
Mr. Harold Bowden Smith, Rugby School.
Mr. J. H. Bowden Smith, Rugby School.
Mr. H. Cave, Ball College.
The Rev. P. Bowden Smith, Rugby.
September 9.
Left here after a week's sojourn, weather not very propitious, rained
almost every day, the rest of the party object to this record.

Rev. Jas. Morris, St Stephens, Haggerston.
Wm. Jas. Morris, Broughton.
James Coulson, Derby.
Rev. Nelson Burrows, St. Augustines Vicarage, Haggerston, London.
Mr. and Mrs. Tyson's kindness and attention have been very much appreciated.

Hamilton Browne, Lewin Rd, Streatham, London.
September 12.
E. O. Mawson, Coopers Hill, Staines, London.
John S. Mawson, The Larches, Keswick.
Stanley Pearson, Manchester.

C. A. Woodward, Norfolk.
September 1 to 12.
We spent a very happy time with Mr. and Mrs. Tyson, who have both treated us with much hospitality and kindness.
S. Lavington Hart, St Johns College, Cambridge.
James Walford Hart, Stoke Newington.
September 14.
Our party, consisting of The Athlete, the festive Sky Pilot, the Q.C. and the notorious Nailes left 'the Laurels', Lakeside, the 'most comfortable, civil and economical quarters' in the Lake District at 7.5 a.m. We arrived at Hawkeshead at 9 a.m. — weather grand — Esthwaite Lake on our right — 12 o'clock brought us to Coniston Head.

It being Sunday, the Sky Pilot insisted on Divine Service, which was held in the Drawing Room at Waterhead Hotel, the servants being summoned. The greatest amateur Athlete in the Three Counties acted as guide on the tour and allowed us egg and milk only, with oatcake, a diet we strongly recommend. The Q.C., raised a technical objection to any heavenward ascent on the grounds that he was especially retained and qualified for going down to hell.

The scenery up to Coniston Head was extremely picturesque, but it grew in grandeur. After diving into a thicket and crossing a stream, we struck the road and started at a good swinging trot for Dungeon Ghyll. We may mention, incidentally for the benefit of tourists, who are not millionaires, that it is advisable, even in farmhouses to ascertain the price of milk and eggs before proceeding to eat them. Reaching Dungeon Ghyll, the Sky Pilot advised us to annoint our feet with oil, which proved a boon and a blessing and worthy of imitation. The Athlete hurried us on to scale the Stake holding us out as a reward, a luscious beef steak at the end of our journey. He himself set a good example, for when he reached the base, he boldly commenced the attack with a run; shot up the precipice like a rocket and was lost to view! We have never seen him since! But understand, that after feeding at Rosthwaite, he walked on to

162

Barrow through the night and turned up there the next morning fresh as paint.

Half way up the rock, the Sky Pilot declared it time for evening service. We accordingly sat down and listened to a few eloquent and ernest appeals to our better feelings, which might have improved the morals, even of William Ruskin. Having previously uncorked a flask of old, unadulterated whisky, he drew largely from nature and the running stream. After singing 'Onward Christian Soldiers', we took the rock at a bound, expecting to find The Athlete waiting for us tarn on the other side, but alas!—no Athlete was there. Nothing, but, a dissolute old roue of a ram.

By following the cairns we found ourselves on the summit of Scawfell. The magnificence of this view rivetted us to the spot and we were only brought to our senses by the shades of night, stealing rapidly around. We had never been here before and felt very much behind. The Sky Pilot, hitherto our moral guide, undertook, in the absence of The Athlete, to be our personal guide, our forebearing and never changing friend, our profound philosopher.

In the darkness of the night he described a stream running through a valley in the far distance. With deep penetration, our philosopher, a borne mountaineer, argued that this stream was a moral stream with a moral purpose and would lead to some good. Relying on him, we plunged into the darkness and finally arrived at the bottom, exhausted, bruised and bleeding at every limb. We here partook of a little carnal enjoyment, by dividing our last oatcake, wondering whether this would be our last meal.

We crossed and recrossed the stream, by this time, discoloured like the flowing Xanthus, with our blood, but lo! Behold! there arises a blessed contrast to the bloody stream, a wicket gate! a glimmering light in the distance!!!

We embraced our Sky Pilot and held a Thanksgiving Service. The very rocks re-echoed again and again the strains of our Evening Hymn. Refreshed, we marched on, eventually arrived here and were cordially entertained at special terms. Retiring to rest by the electric light of a halfpenny, we finally reposed our weary limbs.
-T. Parnell.

T. Chamberlain.

A. Bradlaugh.

Came September 9th. Left September 15th. (For the Scawfell Hotel, Rosthwaite, Keswick). We desire to express our thanks to Mr. and Mrs. Tyson for their very kind attention to us.
W. P. Turnbull, Wolverhampton.
W. H. Hudson, London.
September 17.
C. E. Hanson.
Emily Hanson.
Frank Eastwood.

Annie Eastwood.

Milne Barnsley, Liverpool.
T. W. H. Mitchell, Barnsley.

Julia Sargent.
Walter Sargent.
Kathleen Sargent.
Maud Sargent.
Victoria A. Inglis.
Julia M. Inglis.
Ascended Scawfell Sept. 17th, 1885.
Sella Park-Carnforth.
September 18.
Called here very late last evening, having travelled from Yeathouse
station via Stockhow Hall, Angler's Inn, Gillerthwaite, Black Sail
Pass. We cannot leave without recording our hearty thanks to Mr.
and Mrs. Tyson.
Wilson H. Greacen, Omagh, Ireland.
Samuel W. Greacen,   do
September 21.
Percy L. Pewtrees, Lee, Kent.
September 24 to 25.
Mr. and Mrs. Alfred F. Buxton, London.
Miss E. and B. - Blake, Rugby.
September 24 to 26.
Frederick W. Jackson, Bolton, Lancs.
Henry Hood, Ashbourne.

Mr. and Mrs. W. Frederick Simpson, Kensington, London.
September 28 to 29.
Mrs. Oldham and family, Kensington Park, London W.
Were made very comfortable and met with great kindness and
attention from Mr. and Mrs. Tyson.
September 13 to 25.
George Hastwell, Darlington.
September 29.
8 p.m., October 1st, 10 a.m., Mr. and Mrs. William Andrew of
Edinburgh, came from Buttermere by Scarff Gap and Black Sail and
left for Keswick by Sty Head.
*The home of the Spedding family at Mirehouse on the eastern side
of Bassenthwaite Lake, a few miles north of Keswick, has seen many
famous visitors. Alfred Lord Tennyson and Edward Fitzgerald who
were close friends of James Spedding stayed there in 1835. At the
time Tennyson was involved in creating the epic poem 'Morte
D'Arthur'.*

164

October 3 to 6.
A. L. Pelham and Mrs Pelham, Monmouth.
December 24 to 30.
Fras. E. Wilson, Macclesfield.
H. Wilson, Cambridge.
C. Wilson, Edinburgh.

December 30 to January 2, 1886.
Leonard Wigham, Killiney, County Dublin.
Arnold Wigham,   do
A. Peile, Workington.
A. E. Peile, Workington.
June 15.
Walter Marshall, Surbiton, Surrey (the Dook).
W. H. Holden, London (the Chamois).
W. T. Marshall, Balham, Surrey (Bounder).
July 30.
Ernest E. Lamprell, New Southgate, London.
Climbed Skiddaw this morning and walked on here from Keswick
in the afternoon.
August 9.
Thomas Durley, Birmingham.
From Keswick via Buttermere and Scarff Gap.
August 11.
J. W. Denton, Carlisle.
J. Barnes, Carlisle.
August 20 to 23.
E. M. Déprez; C. Travers; and their little dog Chittabob, all went
to the top of Scawfell and strongly advise other people to go up the
Pike. They found Mrs. Wilson's homestead a very pleasant sojourn.

*This is the end of entries in the Visitors' Books in our possession.
We now include a number of extracts on climbers who were also
visitors to the Tysons, but who have not been previously commented
upon.*

*Alfred Wills is an excellent illustration of the total commitment of
the pioneer climbers. A barrister by profession, Wills visited Row
Farm regularly. However he spent his honeymoon in 1854 in Bernese
Oberland. Here he deserted his new bride for several days, while he
climbed to the summit of the Wetterhorn accompanied by four local
guides.*

*A. F. Mummery also climbed in Lakeland, usually with J. Norman
Collie. In 1895 attempting to climb the Nanga Parbat in the
Himalayas, he disappeared with two Gurkhas during a high level
reconnaissance and was never seen again.*

165

J. Norman Collie was involved in a most controversial incident in the history of British climbing in 1892. This took place on the crags of Scafell. Faced by a holdless wall on the first ascent of a new climb, the leader (Collie) borrowed an ice-axe and hacked out a foothold from the solid rock. It was the first time in Britain that this had happened—the initial use of an artificial aid in rock-climbing. Known as the 'Collie Step' by hundreds of climbers, it is possibly the only foothold in British climbing that has its own name.

With Geoffrey Hastings, A. F. Mummery, and J. W. Robinson, Collie climbed in the Himalayas. He became president of the Alpine Club and chairman of the committee formed to organise the first explorations of Everest. Professor Collie, a scientist who discovered neon, was the first man to take X-ray photographs. He also became one of Europe's outstanding climbers and died in 1942.

Index

Lists references in the introduction, Visitors' Books and explanatory notes of relevance to climbing and fell-walking. The numerous references to Wasdale and the Tyson family are not indexed.